A COLONEL,
A FLAG,
AND
A DOG

by
Cindy Stouffer and Shirley Cubbison

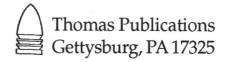

Thomas Publications
Gettysburg, PA 17325

Cover design by Ryan C. Stouch

*Dedicated to the memory
of the
11th Pennsylvania Volunteer Infantry Regiment.*

CONTENTS

FOREWORD

Lieutenant Henry J. Farley pulled the lanyard on a heavy artillery piece at Fort Johnson, South Carolina, and fired into Fort Sumpter on April 12, 1861,[1] the manifestation of differences between the North and South which had been smoldering since the establishment of the American Constitution. To the South, the growth of a strong Federal government was seen as a threat to state sovereignty. Now they were adamant about seceding and forming their own government. Newly-elected President Lincoln, just as determined to preserve the Union, had refused to see South Carolina's representatives to discuss secession. The South saw no recourse but to fight, and the years of dissension finally erupted into gunfire.

On April 15, just three days after the first shot, Lincoln issued a proclamation calling forth "militia of the several States of the Union to the aggregate number of seventy-five thousand."[2] This number would surely be enough to end the open rebellion in three months. Both North and South believed that war would last no longer.

Seeing an opportunity for adventure and, if lucky, a little glory, young men enthusiastically poured forth from all Northern states to join forces and to lick "the rebels." The quota of 75,000 was quickly filled with an overflow of enlistees who were returned to their homes. Pennsylvania did its share with over half of this requisition, supplying 25 regiments.[3]

On April 19, 1861, Major General Robert Patterson of Philadelphia, a veteran of the War of 1812 and the Mexican War, was appointed commander of the Military Department of Washington, which included Maryland, Delaware, the District of Columbia, and Pennsylvania. The Military Department of Washington was shortly after designated the Department of Pennsylvania.[4] It was finally referred to as "Patterson's Army." One of its components and one of the first groups to form in response to Lincoln's call to arms would be designated the Eleventh Pennsylvania Volunteer Infantry Regiment.

The Eleventh Pennsylvania served with distinction during the Civil War. The regiment was formed in the spring of 1861 by Colonel Phaon Jarrett and Captain Richard Coulter. Coulter remained its leader throughout the war, either as regimental or as brigade commander. The courage, determination, spirit, and tenacity of Richard Coulter and the men he commanded became their trademark early in the war and continued to the end. Their mascot, Sallie, became known for her loyalty and devotion to her comrades.

It was somewhat unusual for one regiment to retain throughout the war its commander, its original flag, and its original number, as well as to avoid being dissolved and absorbed into another unit as losses occurred. The Eleventh accomplished all of this.

The Eleventh had several firsts to its credit. Among the first to form in answer to the call for volunteers in 1861, it was again among the first to volunteer for a period of three years. After the three-year period, the men made a ready response to remain for the duration of the war. The troops experienced their first taste of war at Falling Waters, Virginia on July 2, 1861, where they faced Colonel Thomas J. Jackson and Lieutenant Colonel J. E. B. Stuart. After about an hour's fighting, Stuart was repulsed and Jackson withdrew. In this battle a member of the Eleventh was the first Pennsylvanian to give his life's blood for the Union.[5]

Colonel Coulter and his regiment were repeatedly commended for their tough opposition to the enemy on the field. At the Battle of Antietam, September 17, 1862, the unit was fondly referred to as the "Gallant Old Eleventh" by an Indiana regiment who witnessed their conduct in that bloody battle where the Louisiana Tigers made it so hot for the 11th that their brave commander cried for help.

Comparatively little has been written about the Eleventh Pennsylvania Volunteer Infantry. *Story of the Regiment*, by Captain William H. Locke, was published in 1872. Locke, who was the regimental chaplain, included human interest stories–some comical, some somber–but omitted the mascot completely. John Lippy wrote an account of Sallie published in 1962.

According to accounts written by those who knew her, "Sal" played a vital role in the regiment's service to the Union. From the time she joined it in the beginning of the war, the little dog and her regiment were inseparable. She had been transported as a tiny pup onto the fairgrounds of Chester County and never knew anything but army life. From Cedar Mountain to Hatcher's Run, the little bull terrier endured the beatings of battle with no regard for the dangers. Sallie loved the flag, seemed to know what it represented, and proudly followed it onto the fields of conflict. Wherever the boys in blue were, there she would be, enduring all the hardships of a soldier's life. The little dog possessed a healthy contempt for anyone who would flee the front lines, and once, even demonstrated this in a graphic manner.

Life for the Eleventh was not all battle, of course. During the encampments numerous amusing, and sometimes downright hilarious shenanigans took place, which involved Sallie and the boys. Her bright spirit and loving devotion most certainly helped to sustain a good morale and checked the loneliness which was always nagging the soldier away from home. Twice Sallie had the distinct honor of marching in review before President Lincoln.

Before she ever faced a battle, Sallie experienced several life-threatening incidents which demonstrated her incredible luck. Much to the delight of her comrades, Sallie presented them with four "blessed events" during her service in the army. Each event was announced in the Morning Reports. Treated as one of the men, Sallie's comrades referred to her as "more than a mere dog." During the worst of times, when even important baggage had to be left behind, the men of the Eleventh held onto their mascot.

The fate of the flag is traced throughout the war from its presentation to the first bearer in 1861 by Governor Andrew Curtin to the Grand Review in Washington in 1865. Sallie would miss this final glorious event, for her luck ran out two months before Lee's surrender. Uncanny as it may seem, she even prophesied her end by demonstrating an attitude out of character for her. Her pitiful cries prior to her fate were misunderstood until after the fact. After the war the veterans demonstrated their appreciation for Sallie by including her figure on their regimental monument at Gettysburg.

The fighting spirit of the regiment was infectious. Late in the war new recruits who replaced the fallen fought as well as the old veterans. Research has not uncovered information in any source which would indicate that the regiment or any single member of the regiment ever behaved disgracefully on the field of battle.

One might be humbled by the courage and fortitude of Colonel Coulter and his regiment; deeply touched by the amazing stamina and wisdom of their mascot; and thoroughly amused by the occasional antics, all of which have been kept alive in the hearts of storytellers for more than a century. This story is not intended to overshadow the importance of other units or to detail the complete military action of the war in the East. The Eleventh Pennsylvania was only one component of the many thousands of troops who collectively performed their duty with loyalty to their beliefs and with insurmountable courage in the face of death. Some special characteristics of this regiment, however, deserve to be told. This book attempts to bring to life and to pay tribute to the "Gallant Old Eleventh."

ACKNOWLEDGMENTS

With sincere appreciation we acknowledge the assistance of many people who have shared information or helped in other ways: Special thanks to Roy Frampton, author/historian for his historical critique of the manuscript; Anna Jane Moyer, Reference Librarian at Gettysburg College for her diligent search for the meaning of "dageroon;" Tim Smith, licensed battlefield guide at Gettysburg for information on Sallie; Don Markle of Gettysburg for encouragement, advice and counsel; John Burger of Greensburg, Pa., for sharing the Morning Reports on Sallie's litters; Jim Ware, Greensburg, Pa., and Joan Coulter Pittman, Sullivan's Island, S. C., descendants of Richard Coulter, for the 1876 pamphlet, information on James Anawalt, and additional facts about Richard Coulter; Wiley Sword for permission to use the Webster letter and other information; and Pat Tyson of the Clinton County Historical Society for information on Colonel Jarrett.

Thanks also to Suzanne M. Tinsley, Danville, Pa., for information on Amos Zuppinger and other referrals; Randy Hackenburg, of USAMHI, Carlisle, Pa., for information on Amos Zuppinger; Scott Hartwig, Eric Campbell, and Karlton Smith of the Gettysburg National Military Park, for consultation and encouragement; Ted Alexander, Antietam National Military Park, for information regarding Antietam; Norma Donovan, Webster, Ma., descendant of the Edgars, for permission to use their letters.

Thanks also to Don Phanz, Fredericksburg and Spotsylvania National Military Park for referral; Ellen Nelson, Cape Ann Historical Society, Gloucester, Ma., for information on Captain Benjamin Cook; Barbara Joyette, St. John's College, Annapolis, Md., for information; Douglas Cubbison, Madison, Al., for information on railroads; Ernest Shriver, Gettysburg, Pa., for sharing Shriver family history; Judith Andrews, Sharon Morrow, Rosine Bucher, Marilyn Holt, and Judy Wakely for information on Chaplain Locke; and grateful thanks to Joe Ryder for assistance in typing and his encouragement.

Thanks also for the assistance of David Swisher, Alan Aimone, Virginia Gingrich, William Drown, Michael Comeau, Bill Milhomme, Wayne Motts, William A. Hamann, Barbara Cope, Ethel Hinckel, Judith Andrews, Mary Ann Rider, Donna Loubier; volunteers and officers of the Westmoreland County Historical Society; officials of the Pennsylvania Historical and Museum Commission; Latrobe Area Historical Society; and those who assisted at the Adams County Court House.

For all family and friends—extra thanks for their patience during the three years of research and writing required to make this story a reality.

Colonel Richard Coulter.

Colonel Coulter maintained leadership of the 11th Pennsylvania Volunteer Infantry in various capacities from its formation in April, 1861, to the Grand Review in May, 1865.

CHAPTER ONE

"IT WILL ONLY TAKE NINETY DAYS"

In the spring of 1861, Camp Wayne near West Chester, Pennsylvania, was buzzing with activity as men formed the Eleventh Pennsylvania Volunteer Infantry Regiment. From nine counties they came: from the towns of Hazelton, Lock Haven, and Boiling Springs; from Danville, Shamokin, and Greensburg. From farms, coal mines, and lumber mills they gathered to become soldiers. One organizer from Greensburg was Captain Richard Coulter, a Mexican War veteran who would eventually become regimental commander. A pup born during that same spring would soon become part of camp life and part of the regiment for the duration of the war.

Five companies of the 11th Pennsylvania which had been recruited on the West bank of the Susquehanna witnessed an interesting phenomenon: "A few moments before the cars started, and while the soldiers were bidding adieu to their friends, a splendid American eagle flew directly over them, halting momentarily and flapping his wings as though he comprehended the scene below, and then moved on majestically southward amidst the cheers of the crowd."[1]

Phaon Jarrett was unanimously elected colonel of the regiment. Trained at West Point and skilled in engineering, he was eminently qualified to direct the training of troops. Small wonder that the men respected their colonel. In less than ninety days he had made true soldiers of mostly illiterate mountain boys who did not know the left foot from the right.

Camp Wayne was on the former fairgrounds. In the beginning the gathering of the volunteers took on a picnic atmosphere. Families came to watch the soldiers on parade. The men and boys cheered and the ladies strolled about in their best finery. The soldiers enjoyed this attention and greeted all the visitors cordially–especially the many who brought baskets filled with excellent home-cooked food.

One day a man arrived carrying a basket and asking for William Terry of Company I. "Captain Terry, I have the honor to present you with the pup I promised," he said.

"Very good, sir," replied Terry. He peeked inside the basket and smiled. "May I convey my thanks to you on behalf of the members of the regiment."[2] The captain reached in and lifted out a pug-nosed, black-muzzled puppy. Barely four weeks old, when placed on the ground it was just able to toddle about on its short, fat legs.

The bull terrier pup was taken to the quarters of Captain Terry, who made a bed for it under his bunk. Milk and soft bread were secured from the quartermaster. With plenty of eating and sleeping, the little animal thrived. The soldiers named her in honor of two people–a young lady they admired and Colonel Jarrett. The mascot's full name, Sallie Ann Jarrett, was soon shorted to just "Sallie."

The first danger to her came soon after her induction into the regiment. One day during dinner, she suddenly fell, rolled over, and stretched her legs while her whole body trembled convulsively. Everyone thought that they had surely lost their pup. After a gasp and a struggle or two, she survived. Perhaps her eyes had been bigger than her belly, but regardless, she had passed her first crisis, giving an early indication that she might be hardy enough to endure a soldier's life. Eventually Sallie learned to respect the rations, and would lie down among haversacks of meat without disturbing them. She was never seen to touch them again unless the food was offered. When fresh beef was being issued, she would stand without begging until receiving her fair share.

The men grew very fond of Sallie, and would let no one abuse her. Together they learned soldiering. Sallie absorbed the activities of the soldiers: rising at reveille, eating army chow, marching by column or flank, firing muskets, rolling blankets, filling haversacks, sleeping in tents, building breastworks, and living in a large encampment.

After a month of training, the regiment was ordered from Camp Wayne to Maryland to guard the Philadelphia, Wilmington and Maryland Railroad, thus protecting the route to Washington, D. C. This marked the beginning of Sallie's travels with the army. She traveled first-class in the arms of a soldier, in a haversack, or rolled up in a blanket. Sometimes she rode on the baggage wagon. At other times she was transported in the saddlebags of Dr. James Anawalt, the assistant regimental surgeon.[3] She was even known to ride on the back of Richard Coulter's saddle.

One soldier became Sallie's special friend. As the company comic, he had nicknamed himself the "Dageroon." He joked, teased, and laughed to keep up the morale of the troops. He made a special effort to cheer up the lonely and homesick ones. When the regiment was moving, his official position was "baggage guard," but his real assignment was to take care of Sallie. The two became inseparable.

When the 11th passed through Philadelphia, the happy-go-lucky "Dageroon" planned a ridiculous outfit. The baggage wagon contained little to supply his imagination, but he selected an old slouch hat and carried a large knapsack on his back. A railroad lantern dangled from

11

served through entire war until killed at Hatchers Run Vg. 1865

Sal.

The only known photograph of Sallie, the regimental mascot, who spent nearly four years on the battlefields with her comrades.

the knapsack, and around his shoulders he carried several canteens, haversacks, and muskets. Paying no attention to stares and curious glances, the "Dageroon" walked nonchalantly along the sidewalk leading Sallie by a piece of twine. Their passage through Baltimore was much the same, with the soldier stopping to rest here and there and chatting with people who asked him questions about the dog. This Baltimore passage was quite in contrast to a previous scene when Federal soldiers had been attacked by a mob.[4]

Transportation for the regiment had so far been by train, but at Williamsport, Maryland, this ended. For the remainder of their enlistment they went on foot. To ford the Potomac River, Sallie was tied in a feed box on the baggage wagon. Shortly after the crossing, a sharp jolt on the rough road tossed her out and left the poor dog dangling from the short rope. She was gasping and swinging helplessly until one of the baggage guards spotted her and cut her loose. The mascot had barely escaped strangulation, but quickly resumed her place in the wagon. The fortunes of war had to be accepted.

The regiment belonged to a division of the Union Army commanded by Gen. Robert Patterson. They marched toward Martinsburg, Virginia. Battle was imminent, for the Confederate forces at Martinsburg were not likely to let a Union advance go unchallenged. Soon the courage of the Pennsylvanians would be tested for the first time. Nearing Falling Waters, or Hainesville, Virginia, (now West Virginia) on July 2, 1861, Col. John Abercrombie's Brigade, of which the Eleventh was a part, suddenly encountered the brigade of Col. T. J. Jackson, a component of Gen. Johnson's force guarding the Shenandoah. The 11th Pennsylvania, led by Col. Jarrett, was on the right flank facing the infantry and artillery of Jackson's center. When the cavalry of Lt. Col. J. E. B. Stuart attempted to charge the 11th on its right, Col. Jarrett sent three companies to oppose Stuart. Colonel George Henry Thomas' Brigade of the 2nd U. S. Cavalry arrived and moved to the right to threaten Jackson's left flank. The Union held its ground for an hour until Jackson withdrew, realizing that the raw troops he faced were a force to be reckoned with when used effectively by their colonel.

As the battle raged, Amos Zuppinger of Company H in the Eleventh Regiment, became the first Pennsylvanian to die in battle. Private Zuppinger was from Danville in Montour County, Pennsylvania—a German settlement—and might have been a German immigrant. At nineteen years of age he had enlisted in Company H, the "Danville Rifles." Mustered in on April 26, 1861, he was shot in the head on July 2, 1861. Fourth Sgt. Henry C. Parsons of Company A stood near Zuppinger when he fell. He was buried on the field by the Danville Rifles with full military honors. His body was eventually reinterred in the Winchester National Cemetery at Winchester, Virginia, as Amos Sappington.

While Gen. Patterson's army advanced and occupied Martinsburg, rations became short. The army had not yet worked out good supply services, and this presented a new hardship for the men and Sallie. She learned that when the men ate, she ate. When they were hungry, she was hungry.

Many in Martinsburg believed in the Union. One group demonstrated this by giving a handmade national flag to the regiment, honoring them for their part in the Battle of Falling Waters. A gentleman carrying the flag arrived in camp on the evening of July 12, accompanied by a group of fifteen young ladies. One Miss Miller made the presentation:

> In behalf of the ladies of this neighborhood, I am delegated to present to you this flag as a token of their high appreciation of your courage and gallantry in leaving your quiet homes and facing danger and death.... May God bless you, preserve your health and lead you honorably and triumphantly through this contest...then may you be guided safely to your homes, and posterity will...call you blessed that you...endangered your lives to perpetuate our glorious Union....[5]

The ladies had added the words, "11th Rgt. P. V." to the center stripe along with the date of the regiment's organization and the date of presentation.

The flag bearer carried the new flag proudly as the army marched on the next day toward Bunker Hill. Their job was to keep the Confederate forces under Generals Jackson and Johnson in the Shenandoah Valley and unable to threaten Washington. The ashes of the retreating Southerners' campfires were still warm when the 11th camped on the same land.

The next day's march was slower as men filled ditches and moved the felled trees which the Confederate forces had placed in their path. Arriving at Winchester and finding it heavily fortified, Gen. Patterson withdrew his forces to Bunker Hill and then to Charlestown. The 11th had expected to fight; they were ready to fight. In their disappointment, they spit and spoke their opinion of the commanding general as they retraced their line of march. Patterson, however, had been awaiting orders from Gen. Winfield Scott (the general-in-chief), who did not reply to Patterson's July 3 request for orders until July 13.

General Patterson was under pressure by the War Department to advance and attack. General Scott telegraphed him on July 18, 1861: "I have certainly been expecting you to beat the enemy. If not, to hear that

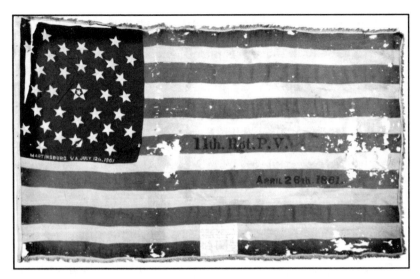

The National Flag presented to the regiment on July 12, 1861, by loyal ladies of Martinsburg, Virginia (now West Virginia). Note the addition of "11th Rgt. P.V." in the center stripe. (Capital Preservation Committee, Harrisburg, PA.)

you have felt him strongly, or, at least had occupied him by threats and demonstrations.... A week is enough to win victories. You must not retreat across the Potomac. If necessary, when abandoned by the short-term volunteers, entrench somewhere and wait for reinforcements."[6]

On the same day Patterson replied from Charlestown. "The enemy has stolen no march upon me. I have kept him actively employed, and by threats and reconnaissances in force caused him to be re-enforced. I have accomplished in this respect more than the General-in-Chief asked or could well be expected, in face of an enemy far superior in numbers with no line of communication to protect."

Still on the same date, Patterson sent another report to Col. E. D. Townsend, Assistant Adjutant General at the War Department:

> With the existing feeling and determination of the three-months' men to return home, it would be ruinous to advance, or even to stay here.... Many of the regiments are without shoes; the Government refuses to furnish them; the men have received no pay, and neither officers nor soldiers have money to purchase with. Under these circumstances, I cannot ask or expect the three-months' volunteers to stay longer than one week.[7]

In another message of July 19, 1861, to the adjutant general, Patterson further stated that, "Almost all the three-months' volunteers refuse to serve an hour over their term, and except three regiments

15

which will stay 10 days, the most of them are without shoes and without pants. I am compelled to send them home, many of them at once."[8]

Among the three ragged regiments agreeing to stay the ten days was the 11th Pennsylvania. With the men in parade formation, the general asked those willing to stay to bring their muskets to shoulder. At the command, "Shoulder arms" every musket went up. Elated at the response, the general rode forward and exclaimed, "With you, my brave Blue Jackets, I can hold this place alone."[9]

On July 25 the regiment left Harpers Ferry by train for Harrisburg to be mustered out on July 31, 1861. Sallie went with them. With them also went Gen. Patterson's official commendation:

> It gives the commanding general great satisfaction to say that the conduct of this regiment has merited his highest approbation. It had the fortune to be in the advance at Falling Waters, where the steadiness and gallantry of both the officers and men came under his personal observation. They have well merited his thanks.

Sallie found herself a member of an outstanding unit. As days went on, the spirit of the dog would match the spirit of the men.

When Col. Jarrett arrived back in Harrisburg for mustering out, he witnessed mobs of angry soldiers clamoring for their pay. Corrupt paymasters were withholding money in an effort to buy the soldiers' claims at a ruinous rate. Colonel Jarrett refused to allow his men to be exploited, and would not permit his regiment to be disarmed until paid. Immediately the men received payment in full and honorable discharge.

During the wait in Harrisburg, Sallie was "dog-napped" by a member of a neighboring unit. She was listed as missing for several days before being rescued. The "Dageroon" made a diligent search until he discovered where she was hidden. Then he retrieved his pal "Sal" and together they made a triumphant march back to company headquarters. Although the "Dageroon" never admitted it, the story around camp was that he had given the soldier responsible for her disappearance a clear understanding that such a thing was never to happen again. The message was delivered, so it was said, with considerably more than verbal emphasis.

Sallie went on furlough to Greensburg with Company I and visited in the homes of several soldiers. During the three months' enlistment, she had escaped death by choking and by strangulation. She had endured being captured and hidden. Her puppyhood had taken her from Pennsylvania to Maryland and into northern Virginia. Now, she was no longer a puppy. Sallie had become a comrade in arms and would continue to share the rigors of army life on weary marches and bloody fields.

CHAPTER TWO

"GOOD DUTY"

The Eleventh returned to Harrisburg in September and reported to Camp Curtin. Some dignitaries in the state capital had decided to redesignate the regiment as the Fifty-first. A new flag bearing the number fifty-one was even prepared, but the men refused to accept it and insisted on keeping their old number. Having distinguished themselves during their initial enlistment, they did not want to lose their identity. Under the banner of the Eleventh they had resisted Jackson and Stuart as the only Pennsylvania regiment to see action in the three-months' enlistment. And under this same flag they had won congratulations from Gen. Patterson and had been accepted by the secretary of war for the second term of enlistment. Eventually, a general order from the governor of Pennsylvania permitted them to remain as the Eleventh; thus, they became the first Pennsylvania regiment to re-enlist for three years' duty.

The dispute over the flag caused the regiment to be held for an extra six weeks as a measure of discipline. The additional drill and training during that time made better soldiers of the men. The atmosphere at Camp Curtin was more serious than it had been at Camp Wayne. The Federal defeat at Bull Run on July 21, 1861, had shown that the war would be, after all, "no picnic."

Several important members of the regiment did not return to service. Colonel Jarrett was not given a new appointment because of his strict political convictions. William Terry, the first owner of Sallie, did not return because he was ill. Terry was from Greensburg and was mustered into service on April 24, 1861, serving as commander of Company I. His records had stated "No evidence of disability" when he was mustered in, but by the time he had completed the three month term of service, his health had deteriorated and ended his military career. George A. Stark, a friend and neighbor who had worked in the woodworking shop where Terry had pursued his trade of coach maker, stated that within a few days of discharge, Terry complained of chronic diarrhea and heart trouble. Stark said that, "He was weak and could not continue work because of his shortness of breathing...he was never fitted for his work after his return home, at his trade or any other manual labor up to the time of his death.... I visited him during his last illness. He was very weak and short of breath and complained of pain over his heart."[1] Terry died in Greensburg on June 22, 1875. He was survived by his wife, Sarah, and two sons aged eight and six.

Sallie's guardian, the "Dageroon," also did not return. He had enlisted in another regiment and was killed by a train on the way to his new unit. The true name of this soldier has never been discovered. In the 1850s the expression "to do dags" meant "to do tricks." The young man might have combined this term with the word "buffoon" to create his unique and popular nickname, the only name recorded by his comrades.

By this time, Sallie was almost six months old and showed a silky brindle coat. Her chest was broad and deep; her head and ears, small. Her eyes were a bright hazel, full of fire and intelligence. The men declared her "a respectable sized dorg!"[2] One member of the 12th Massachusetts wrote:

> The strong attachment of the faithful dog for its master has always seemed to me to involve one of nature's secrets, difficult to explain or understand...Sallie...joined heartily in all the frolics of the soldiers and her temporal well-being was the constant care of a thousand men, as brave and true as any who ever went forth to battle at their country's call. In course of time the Eleventh found itself on the upper Potomac and we men of the Twelfth Massachusetts always regarded ourselves as fortunate in being brigaded with it.
>
> Sallie's acquaintances now became a great deal more numerous.... I never knew [why], but certain it was that at first she was just a little shy of us Massachusetts men. After a while, however, she consented to receive our attentions, and was always sure of a dainty breakfast from any Massachusetts tent into which she poked her nose—that is, if we were not worse off than dogs ourselves.[3]

Sallie made herself part of army life to a degree that made her much more than a mascot. Her entrance into the 11th Pennsylvania in a basket made her the only conscript in an all-volunteer army. As an adult dog, however, she had complete freedom of movement in camp and could have easily moved on; but she did not. The army was her home and the place that she freely chose, making her a true volunteer.

The 11th was sent to Annapolis, Maryland, in November 1861 and was given quarters at St. John's College. There Sallie came into full participation with the regiment. She was among the first to respond when the drum roll called reveille. Many of her comrades appeared with sleepy, unwashed faces and scrambled to line up for roll call while still pulling on trousers or putting on coats. Others entered the grounds with one boot on and the other in hand, all the while grumbling threats against the drummer. They would find Sallie already in line, conveniently attired in her brindle coat. There was something to be said for being a dog!

At squad or company drill Sallie made a habit of selecting a soldier for the day, and followed him patiently until drill was over. Regimental or brigade drill was another matter. There, Sallie took the lead. As units formed, she found the horse of Col. Richard Coulter, the regimental commander. Barking and leaping at the horse, Sallie led it to the drill ground, remaining in front of the horse until the regiment was dismissed.

The Twelfth Massachusetts soldier further wrote:

> The Eleventh Pennsylvania was commanded by one of the bravest men I ever knew–Colonel Richard Coulter...who soon became known throughout the brigade as 'Dick' Coulter, and in course of time we began to speak of Sallie as 'Dick' Coulter's dog.' ...Many a time at dress parade did I go over to the camp of the Eleventh to see the important part that Sallie always took in that imposing pageant. Then with the long line at 'Parade rest' the drum corps slowly marching down the front, the Colonel with folded arms calmly looking into the faces of the men, and Sallie lying still at the feet of the color-bearer, as if she loved to be in the shadow of the flag, the scene was an impressive one. She seemed to understand for what purpose we were gathered there in that strange fashion and men who were not at all superstitious asserted it was their belief that the poor brute was in full sympathy with us in our loyal feeling.... On the march Sallie followed closely behind the Colonel.... When the brigade came into camp the Eleventh was always sure of being represented by a Colonel, a flag and dog.[4]

Two flags comprised the colors of the unit: the national flag given to them at Martinsburg and the regimental flag presented to them by Governor Curtin as a gift of the Commonwealth of Pennsylvania. It was placed in the hands of Sgt. Charles H. Foulke of Company A, who carried it until August 11, 1862. The men saw great symbolism in the dog's position beside the flags that they were pledged to "shield from dishonor with nothing less sacred than your lives."[5] These two positions—to lead off with the colonel's horse when the regiment moved and to front the line at dress parade—were chosen by Sallie at Annapolis and remained her habit until the day she led the column from the camp at Hatcher's Run.

In camp Sallie preferred the captain's quarters, but visited all around. She immediately knew when someone did not belong. The Massachusetts soldier also stated:

In this early period of the war visitors to our camp were plenty. Sallie was always discourteous to outsiders, appearing to have a "holy horror" for civilians, whether ladies, gentlemen, or strange [blacks]. When such entered the camp she would immediately seek the protection of the "boys in blue." Early in her service prisoners of war were conducted through camp, giving the dog a chance to learn that those in the gray uniforms were not her comrades. Ever afterward, Sallie "counter marched" the moment she came within sight of Confederate soldiers.[6]

She had a strong instinct for those she considered to be threatening to her friends. Her actions in camp reflected that instinct.

The regiment remained in Annapolis throughout the winter. In the spring of 1862 Sallie was expecting pups. When she failed to report for roll call one morning, some men began to search. Eventually Sgt. Searcy, an older man in the quartermaster service, located her. At the center of the college grounds stood a fine large tree which was centuries old and was known as the Liberty Tree. At the root of the tree was a decayed section which had created a large cavity. Sallie had chosen this safe and cozy spot for giving birth. This news was announced at headquarters and an entry was made in the Consolidated Morning Report Book of March 7, 1862: Sallie had a litter—nine pups."[7] The sergeant provided a bed of clean straw in an empty room of one of the buildings. Sallie and family were at once moved to these more comfortable quarters.

The men assumed that Sallie would spend most of her time in her new quarters taking care of her young ones. She certainly was not expected to follow soldiers around all day. But Sallie's comrades underestimated her devotion to army life. After her second day of motherhood, she trotted briskly out to the field to resume her duties and made it clear that she intended to stay. In no way could she be coaxed back to her litter while there was work to be done. Often the pups became quite loud in their calling for nourishment, but Sallie made them wait until she was off duty. Because she considered herself a member of the 11th Regiment, she placed her military obligations above her maternal instincts. After all, there was a war going on!

Whenever Sallie had pups her behavior was always the same–duty to the Union came first, duty as a mother second. If the army marched, she marched with it. If the pups were too small to march, they were carried in a box in the baggage wagon. If they were able to march, they

The Liberty Tree on St. John's College campus, Annapolis, Maryland. Sallie had her first litter of pups in a cavity in the trunk of this tree.

(Photo by Shirley Cubbison)

Close-up of the Liberty Tree showing that the cavity is now filled in with 55 tons of concrete, iron, and bricks in an effort to preserve it.

(Photo by Shirley Cubbison)

did so. Many a soldier must have been cheered or been distracted from the thoughts of an impending battle by the sight of Sallie marching along with four or five pups trailing behind.

Always the men of the quartermaster department made sure the pups were cared for. At various times each one was placed in a suitable home in Pennsylvania, New York, Maryland, or Massachusetts.

At Annapolis the regiment had been assigned to guarding the railroad, providing provost guard throughout the city, and completing work details at the National Naval Academy. In spite of the unit's reputation as a good fighting regiment, some men would behave like undisciplined boys on their off-duty hours. Colonel Coulter took quick action to curb such problems:

St. John's College, Annapolis, Md.
January 14th, 1862,

Order No. 3.

Complaint having been made to these headquarters on the part of the citizens of Annapolis that a large Oak-tree [Tulip poplar] standing at the northeast end of the college green is being injured by shooting at it and otherwise. The officers and men of this regiment are hereby forbidden to mutilate or injure any of the trees in the Green and especially the one referred to or permit the same to be done by breaking the branches, removing the bark, shooting at or committing any nuisance about the same. A violation of this order will be promptly and severely punished.

By order of R. Coulter, Col. Commdg.

❖ ❖ ❖ ❖

Annapolis, Md.
January 29th, 1862

Order No. 10.

...2. A very serious accident having occurred in the regiment today in consequence of men passing through quarters with bayonets fixed upon their muskets–hereafter no soldier will pass in through or out of quarters with bayonets fixed on muskets. When in quarters bayonets shall invariably be unfixed. Non-commissioned officers will see that this order is strictly complied with and any violation of it will be severely punished.

By order of R. Coulter, Col. Commdg.[8]

Lack of personal cleanliness was another problem which the colonel had to address:

St. John's College, Annapolis, Md.

Order No. 33.

1st. The surgeon having reported that much of the sickness in the regiment arises from the extreme uncleanliness in person and clothing of many of the men. In order to remedy this evil all company commanders are required forthwith to inspect the persons and clothing of their men. And to compel when necessary immediate cleansing and where the soldier shall refuse or neglect to tend to such orders, the officer shall have the same thoroughly performed by a detail in charge of a noncommissioned officer.

2nd. In the future officers will make frequent inspections of the quarters, cooking utensils, clothing and persons of the men and enforce the necessary policing and washing.

By order of R. Coulter, Col. Commdg.

❖   ❖   ❖   ❖

Special Orders No. 6.

1. Companies A. C. D. F. and H. and the Regimental Band will each detail five men for police duty to report to Capt. Kuhn of Company A at his quarters at 2 o'clock P. M. this day.

2. Captain Kuhn is directed with the above detail to thoroughly police all the buildings occupied by the regiment, requiring all baggage to be taken from the room, and have the quarters thoroughly cleansed.

❖   ❖   ❖   ❖

February 3rd, 1862

...The regimental soldiers have today been examined by Surgeon McAnnulty medical inspector for this department and with a most mortifying result.

He reports the quarters filthy and many of the men both ragged and dirty. He moreover remarked their utter inattention and apparent ignorance in matters of Courtesy and Soldierly bearing toward officers.... Knapsacks shall be packed every morning immediately after reveille roll call and together with all the other property, shall be carefully arrayed in the rooms. Spittoons shall be placed in all the rooms.

R. Coulter, Col. Commdg.[9]

In army terms the time at Annapolis was "good duty," but a soldier is always moving on. For the 11th the orders to move came on April 9. The eight hundred men with tents, baggage, and quartermaster provisions were loaded onto railroad cars. At sundown the train pulled out just as the heaviest snow storm of the season engulfed them and caused the train to stop on the tracks for the night. This was unusual for Maryland but it seemed just like home to the men from Pennsylvania. The warm April sun melted the snow in the morning and they continued toward Washington, D. C.

While quartered in Washington, the regiment was full of rumors about their next assignment. A soldier hates the uncertainty of what lies ahead more than he hates the danger. One event in Washington took their thoughts off the rumors and gave the 11th a memorable honor. Colonel Coulter received a special invitation to march his regiment to the White House and pass in review. William Locke, the regimental chaplain, recalled the event:

Standing on the steps of the Executive Mansion, as we saw him in the clear light of that 15th of April, with head uncovered and a kindly smile playing before him, is ...our most vivid recollection of Abraham Lincoln.[10]

Sallie participated in this special honor.

The next day, the regiment boarded boats for Alexandria, Virginia and from there went to Manassas by rail. Ahead lay the Battle of Cedar Mountain.

CHAPTER THREE

"BLIZZARD OF FIRE"

Manassas Junction in April 1862 was a destroyed village surrounded by miles of charred camp equipment left behind by Confederate forces. It reflected the bitter struggle for control of the routes leading to Richmond and to Washington.

The 11th Pennsylvania was guarding the Manassas Gap Railroad with its companies deployed at While Plains, Broad Run, Thoroughfare Gap, Haymarket, and Gainesville. This was similar to their duty at Annapolis, but much more vigilance was needed in Virginia, hostile territory for Union forces. Those on picket duty needed the sharp hearing of a rabbit and the keen eyes of a hawk.

In May Col. Coulter received orders to move the regiment to Catlett Station and then to Falmouth, Virginia. The men were once again going on foot, sometimes covering thirty miles a day. Those were weary, footsore miles sometimes on roads made almost impassable by the rain, and on other days, 100 degree heat. On the march Sallie always followed closely behind the colonel unless restrained. No matter how many of the men fell out during such long marches, she never straggled. She seemed to disregard hunger, thirst, and exposure to sun or rain.

The summer of 1862 found the 11th Pennsylvania as part of Brig. Gen. James Rickett's Division, criss-crossing northern Virginia with battles at Cedar Mountain and Thoroughfare Gap. Both were part of the Second Bull Run campaign. They were at Aquia Creek, Manassas, Gainesville, Culpeper, Warrenton, and Front Royal. At Front Royal they bivouacked by the light of flashing lightning after marching in a violent rainstorm. They forded rivers and built bridges. At one crossing of the Shenandoah River the regiment was the rear guard and escorted the last detachment across just a few moments before the bridge was swept away by the raging waters.

On August 9, 1862 Union and Confederate forces clashed at Cedar Mountain, Virginia. In 1883 Philip Faulk, a veteran of the 11th and corporal of Company F, wrote of the battle:

> Early on the morning of August 4, 1862 Rickett's Division struck tents at Waterloo and then began Pope's [Maj. Gen. John Pope, commander of the Union Army of Virginia] forward movement toward Culpeper on the road to Gordonsville. Pass-

ing through a region of natural beauty and adorned with stately mansions the division bivouacked, after the first day's march, at the old South Fork Church near Robertson's River.... Toward evening Hartsuff's Brigade [Brig. Gen. George Hartsuff] composed of the Eleventh Pennsylvania, Twelfth and Thirteenth Massachusetts, and Ninth New York National Guard, pitched tents near the town of Culpeper. Our march had been extremely toilsome, owing to extreme sultriness, the glaring beams from a fiery sun having poured down upon us from a cloudless sky from early morn. The 7th of August passed without unusual interruption of the quiet of our temporary camp, but on the 8th an order was issued from headquarters directing the division to advance immediately. It was known that Stonewall Jackson had already crossed the Rapidan, his advance lines having skirmished with our cavalry scouts. The lines were evidently contracting and slowly but surely approaching the crisis of battle.

In obedience to the order during the afternoon of the 8th we abandoned our camp and proceeded through Culpeper toward Pony Mountain, in the vicinity of which we bivouacked for the night. The moon looked down upon our white tents and myriads of stars gemmed the sky. It was to be the last night on earth for many in both armies, for the morrow would send sorrow to homes amid the green hills of New England as well as others toward the Gulf. Never a sun rose brighter and never did nature smile more serenely than upon the morning of the 9th of August. While the dust yet lay clogged with the night damp, lines of flashing steel sprang from the bivouac into "magnificently stern array." The word of command, the bugle blast and the tap of drums marshaled the lines of battle. Rapidly formed ranks pressed forward, and diverging into the main roads the forest-crowned summit of Cedar Mountain rose into full view. Slowly the vapors dispersed, disclosing the openings in the deep mountain foliage, where the sunbeams penetrated and flashed upon the enemy's artillery.

Our columns finally halted in the open fields and along the wayside and waited long after noonday, while regiment after regiment of General [Nathaniel] Banks' command hurried by to engage again the veterans of Jackson. For hours those regiments filed by, enthusiastic and eager for battle. Their banners bore the marks and scars of Luray, Winchester, Cross Keys and Port Republic and had followed the "Mountain Devil" Jackson far up the valley. The troops of our division still rested on their arms, waiting to be called forward to mingle in the work. This suspense was worse than all the excitement of actual battle. At length, late in the afternoon, the boom of artillery vibrated heavily upon the air and awoke the slumbering echoes. The earth seemed to recoil with rapid concussions. For two hours the thunders of battle rolled up in our front in loud, deep meaning volumes not three miles distant. Banks was confident of success without the assistance of McDowell [Maj. Gen. Irwin McDowell], and therefore, our division remained inactive in the rear until Jackson was reinforced by Hill's Corps, eight thousand strong, which falling with the fury of whirlwind upon the exhausted ranks of Banks, caused them to waver and give away.

It was now that Banks called for aid, and in hearty response Ricketts' Division sprang into advancing lines. Hastily dispensing with knapsacks, the division swept forward. Suddenly the battlefield burst into full view. Approaching still nearer the cheers of the combatants were distinctly heard, mingled with the metallic peals of the deep-throated cannon and the sharp detonations of volleyed musketry. At this juncture Generals Pope and McDowell rode along our line and were greeted with cheers at every point....

The wounded now appeared, begrimed with dust and powder, toiling toward the rear. In many cases ghastly wounds, from which red streams dyed the grass at every step, portrayed vividly the horrible realities of war. The scene was one of indescribable excitement. The brigade continued to advance down the long inclined plane. In the west the sun was sinking behind the outline of the Blue Ridge, while in the east the broad, round disc of the moon, blood red, rose upon the scene. Moving on through roads that were almost entirely blockaded by ambulances, gun carriage, streams of wounded, musicians, teamsters and stragglers, who surged hither and thither in confused masses toward the rear, it became evident that we were about to confront the enemy. Such exclamations as these fell upon the ears: "Forty-sixth Pennsylvania cut to pieces!" "Eighth Connecticut wiped out!" "Give them merry hell, boys!"

As we proceeded the drum corps of the Eighty-eighth Pennsylvania played a march–"Dixie"–and as the music swelled into martial strains the division swept forward until the crest of a long naked ridge was gained, when the gleaming of our arms revealed to the eager enemy our position. Our lives momentarily faltered and the music suddenly ceased. Captain Shurtleff of the Twelfth Massachusetts, a graduate of Yale, fell beneath this fire. Quickly rallying, the brigade again moved forward in compact column, and wheeling into position under the cover of the crest of a knoll on the ground previously occupied by Banks' right, swung into position in column by division. The enemy's shells hissed through the air like winged demons, forming a picture grand and terrible. In their screaming course streaks of light lingered across the sky and the pale blue smoke hung almost motionless high in the air. Nearly every shot and shell, owing to an incorrect range, passed over us and striking among the branches of trees in the wood beyond crushed them down with a terrific noise.

Suddenly the harsh whirr of wheels was heard. [Captain James] Thompson's [Battery C, Pennsylvania Independent Light Artillery] was deploying into position on our left. In a moment afterwards the battery was at work. A desultory fire was the only reply, and in fifteen minutes the enemy's advanced battery was silenced. Their repulse had been complete, and with one dismounted gun, thirteen horses and ten men killed they hastily retired to their main line. General Hartsuff at this time rode along our brigade line, exhorting the men to stand firm and when engaged to "keep cool and fire low." Again the cannonading opened from fresh artillery, in position on the side of Cedar Mountain, but in the indistinct light the enemy failed to obtain an accurate range, and their shot consequently passed overhead back into the forest depths. Late in the night their firing ceased altogether, save the sharp report of the rifles in the deadly skirmish. The midnight silence was broken at intervals by the moans of the dying and the neighing of wounded horses. Occasionally the unearthly braying of mules sounded back from where the white-topped ammunition wagons appeared above the pines, and told plainly that they shared in the agitation of the night.

The vigils were at length ended. The sun rose brightly. The dead lay where they fell, and with glazed eyes, stony and upturned faces formed a painful picture of terrible war. All was again calm, almost as the silent dead, and only the repulsive wreck of the conflict remained to remind the living of the carnage of the past and point them to the prospects of the future. The Confederates had fallen back during the night, after their severe repulse by Rickett's Division, and there was no disposition manifest on their part to renew the conflict, inasmuch as they applied for an armistice to bury their dead. This was granted, and in accordance with the usage, details from both armies were soon employed in performing the last rites for the remains of the fallen. While in the discharge of this duty one party, at some distance from the scene of the main struggle, came upon the body of a Union soldier who lay with a shattered musket clutched tightly in his hands, while around him lay the dead bodies of nine Confederates. Other evidence of the desperate and sanguinary character of the conflict were presented in the numerous carcasses of horses, broken fragments of artillery caissons, articles of clothing, knapsacks, muskets, and the prostrate forms over which the cavalry made charges. Nearly four thousand men were killed and wounded in this most desperate battle.[1]

So ended the Battle of Cedar Mountain. Sallie had continued to "lead" the regiment on the march, although she was customarily sent to the rear of the line when a battle began. At Cedar Mountain she was no longer content to be in the last line. True to her feisty terrier nature, she took an active part in the short but bloody battle. Now a tried and true soldier, she had been with the army long enough to see her boys in blue wounded and killed. She wanted to stay with her comrades, and she insisted on staying close to the flag just as she had done at dress parade. It was a dangerous position, for every unit tried to shoot down or capture the colors of the opposing force. Sergeant Charles H. Foulke of Company A, who had carried the flag for almost a year, was wounded in the foot, and the flag passed to Sgt. Robert H. Knox of Company C. Sallie remained at the front though the air was full of missiles and the ground almost trembled beneath her feet. The men fired and Sallie barked! She continued to show this spirit at Rappahannock Station, Second Bull Run, Chantilly, South Mountain, and other engagements.

On August 28 Rickett's Division was ordered to Thoroughfare Gap to prevent Maj. Gen. James Longstreet's forces from joining Brig. Gen. "Stonewall" Jackson at Bull Run. They marched in haste through fenced lots, woods and fields. One man remembered that, "There were no songs or jests and even the chronic grumblers were still.... The only sounds were the steady footfalls of the column and the tinkling noise made by bayonets striking the tin cups fastened to the haversacks."[2] The 11th led Rickett's Division because they were already familiar with this narrow, rocky pass in the Bull Run Mountains. Pushing up the hill against severe fire, they established a line on the eastern ridge. As artillery was difficult to use in the steep terrain, it was a musketry battle with sound echoing between the hillsides like cannon fire. The regiment held its position for four hours at great cost before withdrawing to join the rest of Gen. McDowell's Corps at Bull Run.

Colonel Fletcher Webster, commander of the 12th Massachusetts, in a letter to his wife on August 30 described a portion of the battle at Thoroughfare Gap:

We marched to Thoroughfare Gap where the enemy was expected to try and pop through. We got there after a hard march Wednesday about three P. M. Our brigade was in advance. On getting near the gap, our brigade was sent forward skirmishing and as support to Matthews' Battery.... On each side the gap, which is just wide enough for a carriage road, rise high, steep, thickly wooded hills. Just at the mouth of the gap on the eastern side there is a small space, for building, and there are some stone houses and a large stone mill. We approached the gap from the east, so these buildings were on our right. Coulter with the Eleventh Pennsylvania supported by the New York 9th had the right, the Twelfth and Thirteenth the left of the advance. No sooner had we got within a short distance than the enemy, concealed in the woods and stone buildings, opened. On the right Coulter had a sharp fight. The buildings were too strong for him. He fought like a hero, but was obliged to fall back and with the 9th retired up the road to the rear. He lost two officers and sixty men.[3]

The action at Bull Run on August 30 was disastrous for the Union. Colonel Coulter's horse was killed by a shot in the neck. Sallie had led this horse to the parade ground many times. Sergeant Robert H. Knox of Company C was severely wounded, losing his right leg, and the flag passed on the field into the hands of 1st Sgt. Samuel S. Bierer, Company C, who was immediately wounded. Second Lt. Absalom Schall of Company C took the flag but was severely wounded. It was again taken by Sgt. Bierer, who carried it to Centerville. The regimental flag was saved, but Sgt. William Feightner, carrying the national flag, was wounded and captured. The flag given by the ladies of Martinsburg fell to the hands of the 17th Virginia.

Colonel Webster died in this battle. He was in front of the 12th Massachusetts, gesturing with his sword when the right wing of Col. Montgomery D. Corse's Brigade of Virginians broke through the remnant of the 11th Pennsylvania. Webster was instantly shot in the arm and chest and fell heavily. Several men tried to assist him and finally an officer and a squad of men were sent for a physician. The doctor arrived in time to witness Webster breathing his last. In the letter he had written earlier that day he had told his wife that it might be his last.[4] This brigade commander was held in high esteem, as was his famous father, Daniel Webster. In his place, Col. Coulter took command of the brigade.

May 16, 1862, marked the beginning of the close association between the 11th Pennsylvania and the 12th and 13th Massachusetts regiments. The history of the 13th Massachusetts states: "The Eleventh Pennsylvania joined our brigade today. Hartsuff's brigade, as now formed, consists of the Ninth New York, ...the Eleventh Pennsylvania, and the Twelfth and Thirteenth Massachusetts, and these regiments continued together in the same division during the remainder of our service, and for many months we were together in the same brigade, an unusual circumstance, we believe.[5]

In all these battles and troop movements Sallie always knew her own regiment. No one could fully understand how she could distinguish the 11th from all others. She could even recognize the teamsters who drove wagons for the regiment, even though she seldom saw them. Once when the army crossed a river, Sallie missed crossing with her men. Realizing this, she located the wagon that belonged to headquarters and stayed with it until it arrived in camp. There she trotted over to her own quarters. Even though an entire corps, as many as 10,000 troops, might pass by her, she never mistook the 11th, and never followed any other.

First Sergeant Sam Bierer (left), flag bearer, and his brother, Captain Jacob Bierer of Company C, 11th Pennsylvania Volunteer Infantry. Both were wounded at Second Bull Run. Sam was also wounded at Antietam. Both were discharged in 1864. (Latrobe Area Historical Society)

CHAPTER FOUR

"FOR GOD'S SAKE...HELP US... "

On September 17, 1862,–under cloudy skies with a temperature of 70 degrees–Union and Confederate forces clashed at Antietam Creek near Sharpsburg, Maryland, in the bloodiest one-day battle of the war. General Robert E. Lee was determined to invade the North. Lee's orders, intercepted by the Union, revealed the railroad center at Harrisburg, Pennsylvania, to be his ultimate objective. Lee was compelled to turn and face Maj. Gen. George B. McClellan's army which was moving rapidly northward behind Lee.

General Jackson's division commanders, Brig. Gen. John Bell Hood and Maj. Gen. D. R. Jones were positioned in the woods west of the Hagerstown Pike near the Dunker Church. Major Gen. Joseph Hooker's First Corps was on the Union right and was sent into a forty-acre field about three o'clock on Tuesday afternoon, September 16. There it was fired upon by the Confederates. Both armies lay on their arms during the night. At first light of the 17th, ranks of armed men sprang up throughout the corn field and the nearby woods. Back and forth fought the blue and the gray, each alternately advancing and then being forced back. Gaping holes appeared in every line as it advanced, while the field was raked by artillery. The first Union advance had been successful, but short-lived. As the broken Union line streamed back, Gen. Hooker sent a message to Gen. Ricketts: "Send me your best brigade." Hartsuff's Brigade came downhill on the double-quick past the fragments of three brigades in retreat. At the moment of entering the cornfield Hartsuff fell severely wounded, and Col. Coulter took command of the Third Brigade.

As the battle raged, a deadly charge by the Louisiana Tigers sent Col. Coulter's men back through the cornfield and to the edge of the East Woods. There they rallied and held on under what a member of the 12th Massachusetts labeled "the most deadly fire of the war."[1] As Locke described it:

> The whole line crowned the hill and stood out darkly against the sky: But lighted and shrouded even in flame and smoke. There for half an hour they held the ridge, unyielding

in purpose, exhaustless in courage. There were gaps in the line, but it nowhere bent. Their supports did not come, and they were determined to win without them. They were there to win that field....

John Brenahan of the 27th Indiana observed:

This gallant little regiment was drawn up in line in the southeast corner of the field, near the timber, and about 75 yards in front of where the 27th halted. [The 11th was] FIGHT-ING LIKE DEVILS and cheering Brigadier General George H. Gordon's brigade as it advanced and formed a line in the rear. As soon as these troops had filed past, the three regiments of the brigade in line were ordered to fire, which was done in good order, bringing the enemy to a stand within 300 yards of our line. The firing on both sides was very heavy, and must have continued for more than two hours without any change of position on either side.[2]

As Colonel Lyle of the 90th Pennsylvania regiment advanced through the East Woods, "Coulter hurried back from the front line, found Lyle and called out, 'For God's sake come and help us out!' Coulter's wrecked formations were pulled back and Lyle's men took their places."[3]

Private Daniel Matthews of Company C, who had carried the flag since Centerville, was severely wounded. The flag was taken by Pvt. William Welty, Company C, who was killed almost immediately. Corporal Frederick Welty, Company C, took the flag but was soon severely wounded also. The flag remained on the field for some time, all of the men near it having been killed or wounded. It was then taken up by 2nd Lt. Edward H. Gay of Company F, who received two gunshot wounds and passed the flag to Sgt. Henry Bitner of Company E, who managed to carry it to the end of the action.

Sallie had gone into the cornfield with one of the skirmishers. He tried to chase her back, but she refused to go. A minie ball struck her on the side, but still she would not leave the field until the battle was over. Fortunately, the ball had only made a mark through her hair. The soldier's concern for Sallie could have stemmed partly from the fact that she was again expecting puppies.

As evening fell, the field remained in both Union and Confederate hands. Half of the 11th Pennsylvania lay dead or wounded: one officer and twenty-six men killed, 4 officers and eighty-five men wounded, with two taken prisoner. Of the Third Brigade's eleven hundred men who had entered the cornfield only five hundred returned. Only a fragment of the 12th Massachusetts remained to carry back its regimental colors. They suffered 67% casualties–more than any other unit on the field. The Louisiana Tigers suffered losses almost as high, with 61% casualties.[4] Squads of surgeons and chaplains searched the field for any of the wounded who might have lived through the carnage. Locke wrote:

> But that field, furrowed by cannon shots and strewed in every direction with human forms, was a place of the dead. Cries of–water!–water!–uttered in tones of beseeching agony fell upon our ears in the first hours of the battle. Now every tongue was still and every heart had beat its last pulsation.
>
> Death came to many with musket raised to the shoulder in the very act of firing; and in falling forward, the dead soldier kept fast hold of his gun. Others, again, lay on the ground with arms wide extended and the last look of anguish fixed in the rigid features. In a single row with scarcely two feet between them were eighty-one of the enemy's dead. It was a battle line moving forward, each man meeting death at the same instant. Such a volley, telling so fearfully on the front rank, was a complete check at that point; for there were no indications here of advance and retreat, as were seen on other parts of the ground, in the bodies of friends and foe falling together.
>
> The tired survivors lay on their arms in line of battle. "Neither side would admit defeat; neither would claim victory."[5]

General Lee, realizing that McClellan was receiving strong reinforcements and that another counter-offensive would be suicidal, withdrew on the evening of September 18 and the morning of September 19.

Sallie showed great sympathy for the wounded. One of the soldiers said that, "Sallie came and licked their wounds."[6] Her role that day had been not only to fight, but to comfort and to make a dog's attempt to heal.

The army encamped near Sharpsburg during October. Such a camp was set up in an orderly pattern. Streets were laid out in straight lines. Tents were in double rows facing outward so that each faced its own company street. Drainage ditches were dug, and the streets were cleared so that everything presented a neat appearance. Notwithstanding the effort toward making the camp appear like any ordinary town, it lacked certain comforts of home. As mentioned by Chaplain William Locke:

> We could wish that all things that crawl but to contaminate and annoy might be kept in secessia.... But even in this loyal State of Maryland there are all sorts of creeping worms and flying bugs. They make of one's body, during the night season, a common highway. Just at that delightful moment...when

the...world is fading into that out of which dreams come, did you ever have one of those long-legged spiders take the dimensions of your face? Or a black beetle persist in getting into your ear, while half a dozen over-large ants, mistaking your nose for an anthill, make a violent effort to stop up the channel through which you draw your ration of oxygen? Then you never made your bed on the ground overlooking the Potomac in the State of Maryland.[7]

Chaplain Locke might well have added: "Did you ever see a dog scratch endlessly, snap viciously at a bug, bite its tail or turn round and round searching for a comfortable spot?" On October 20, 1862, while in this miserable situation, Sallie had her second litter—ten pups. By the end of the month the army left Sharpsburg and moved southward, with the 11th giving special attention to Sallie and her new brood.

Sergeant Steele Williams and his son, Walter S. Williams, of Company F, 11th Pennsylvania Volunteer Infantry. Sergeant Williams was discharged on February 6, 1863 for wounds. Walter, a muscian, was mustered out with the company on July 1, 1865. (Pennsylvania State Archives)

CHAPTER FIVE

"REBIRTH OF AN ARMY"

In early November Maj. Gen. George McClellan of the Union Army, now called the Army of the Potomac, was replaced by Maj. Gen. Ambrose Burnside. Burnside was determined to capture the city of Fredericksburg, Virginia, on the Rappahannock River. His plan involved crossing the river on pontoon bridges. The Union Army would then capture and fortify Marye's Heights, a high bluff overlooking the river and the city. Nothing went according to plan. The pontoons did not arrive when expected, and during the delay the Confederate forces were able to place artillery and rifle pits on the heights.

Major Gen. George G. Meade's Division crossed the river on December 11, established a line by afternoon, and lay under arms throughout the night. On the morning of the 12th Reynold's Corps crossed and with Meade formed the Union left. On the morning of December 13 a thick fog covered everything, allowing only one yard of visibility. When it lifted, the Union left advanced, facing both Confederate infantry and concentrated cannon fire of Jackson's Corps. Lines of blue seemed to melt away.

The 11th had not filled its ranks since the Battle of Antietam and numbered only one hundred eighty officers and men. Their flag bearer, Corp. John V. Kuhns of Company C, was three times severely wounded, losing his left leg. The next bearer was Pvt. Cyrus W. Chambers, of Company C, who was killed. Corporal John W. Thomas, also of Company C, who picked up the flag, was next to be severely wounded. The flag was brought off the field by Capt. Benjamin F. Haines of Company B. Colonel Coulter was badly wounded and carried from the field. The ranks were thinned and broken. Brigade after brigade was hurled against the entrenched Confederates. Locke gives details of this action:

> The quiet hills, no longer concealed by the fog, were seen to be filled with cannon, enfilading every foot of the plain; while from behind the railroad embankment, and from the woods beyond, the double lines of rebel infantry discharged their rifles in the face of our advancing columns. The enemy

had now revealed himself, and firing over the heads of our own men, who were ordered to lay close to the ground, a hundred cannon from Stafford Hights [*sic*] were turned upon those woods and hills.

An hour of such work as made the very earth to shake, and fill the air with fiendish sounds, was followed by a moment of quiet. It was the signal for a renewal of the advance. The plain was again a sheet of flame, as if ten thousand muskets had been discharged by a single touch. Again those reticent woods were sending forth sounds of death. But the Third Brigade moved steadily forward, followed by the Second and the First, within a few yards of the railroad.

The Eleventh was on the extreme left of the first line, and moving obliquely toward the railroad, encountered the concentrated fire of the enemy.... Before the railroad was reached eight of the regiment killed and seventy-three wounded, including the colonel and five other officers, marked the ground over which we had passed.

Through the ranks of the Third Brigade came Colonel Lyle, at the head of the Second Brigade, charging against the weakened line of the enemy across the railroad, and into the woods in front; while the First Brigade further to the right, making a similar move, penetrated the enemy's line, capturing two hundred prisoners. The Pennsylvania Reserves, on the left of Gibbon's Division, were equally successful in breaking through the lines of A. P. Hill, and throwing them back on those of Early. Reinforcements were needed to hold the advantage we had gained, and to press the yielding rebels still more furiously. But reinforcements did not come. The enemy was quick to see the delay; and massing his forces at the threatened point, compelled us to abandon the ground so dearly bought, and that we ought to have held secure.

It was late in the afternoon; and falling back across the Bowling Green Road, the Eleventh took a position near the bivouac of the previous evening. Darkness ended the strife, and hill and plain, so recently thundering with artillery, and rattling with the sound of the exploding muskets, were wrapt in the silence of night....

To the Chaplain of the Eleventh was assigned the duty of keeping a general record of the deaths, and burying the dead. A spot of ground near the house was made sacred as the cemetery of our companions; and with all the care and skill displayed by the surgeons, the performance of our solemn duty was painfully frequent.

Dig deep boys," said the corporal in charge of grave diggers. "The old man that owns this ground won't have much respect for these graves after we leave. He may level them down, but we'll show him that he can't reach the bodies.[1]

Sallie's usual conduct on the fields of battle took a turn at Fredericksburg. With so few members of the 11th remaining on the field, finding her own comrades became more and more difficult. Strictly loyal to the 11th and shy among strangers, Sallie thought the situation called for an about-face. Off the battlefield she would have done the same thing if she could no longer have recognized her boys. "Old Daddy Johnson" who was attached to the hospital service saw her and whistled. He described her as having a "drooping tail and humbled crest."[2] Sallie was fond of Johnson and often followed him, but instead of going to him, she gave a glance of recognition and hurried on across the bridge. Looking for the place where the 11th had been earlier, she did not stop until she reached the temporary hospital on the other side. It was a spot to which many of her comrades would soon be carried. Captain Benjamin Cook of the 12th Massachusetts described Sallie as being demoralized. In this, he applied a soldier's, not a dog's, viewpoint, for Sallie had turned away not because of enemy fire, but because of her separation from the regiment. In a few hours the rest of the division pulled back to the river in retreat, and some men declared that it would have been better for the Union Army if they had followed the dog's example earlier.

Action on the Union right had been equally disastrous. Forces under Generals Hancock and Howard were ordered against Confederate forces strongly entrenched behind a stone wall and under the cannons on Marye's Heights. The blue lines "fell like leaves in an autumn wind."[3] General Ambrose Burnside ordered brigade after brigade against the stone wall. One soldier described it: "They reach a point within a stone's throw of the stone wall...that terrible stone wall. No farther. They try to go beyond, but are slaughtered. Nothing could advance farther and live."[4] Even a Confederate officer who stood on Marye's Heights after the battle allegedly remarked, "I am looking at the enemy, but what a useless waste of humanity." More than twelve thousand Union men were dead, wounded or missing. Despite this loss, Burnside was prepared to order a second attack on the following morning but was dissuaded by the corps commanders. Two days later Burnside reluctantly withdrew all his forces across the river.

Sallie's canine instinct had made a better assessment of the situation than did the army commander. General Burnside had great personal courage, but he had stubbornly ordered men into battle against an insurmountable enemy position. Sallie's action did not cause her to lose the high esteem of the men. General Burnside, however, was relieved of command a month later. But before that took place, Burnside and the Virginia winter had more in store for the Army of the Potomac.

The army withdrew to the vicinity of Falmouth, Virginia. The men assumed they would be in quarters for the winter and began to build winter huts. In mid-January Burnside decided to seek another attack route and ordered the army upstream along the Rappahannock. Colonel Coulter went along by ambulance but was forced to turn back because he had not sufficiently recovered from his wounds. That wagon was the last for a while to successfully move. The regiment was about to experience another setback, the infamous Mud March. Three days of icy rain turned the Virginia sand and clay soil into a bottomless pit. Infantry soldiers and horsemen struggled to wade ahead. Supply wagons, caissons, and ambulances were mired above the hubs. Double and triple teams were used to pull cannon, but the horses were paralyzed in mud up to their bellies. The Confederates encamped on the opposite bank of the Rappahannock observed the Union's plight and catcalled across the river, "Burnside's stuck in the mu-u-u-d."[5] The army moved only one mile in a day compared to the usual pace of twelve miles in one day. Finally the men straggled back to camp to complete their dugout-and-log huts.

A totally demoralized army settled down for the winter. The men had lost confidence in their generals, in themselves, and even in the cause of the Union. Desertions increased by the hundreds. Letters from home said that the war was unpopular in the North, that it might be time to compromise with the South and put an end to the war "here and now." The announcement that Maj. General Joseph Hooker had been appointed commander of the Army of the Potomac brought little reaction from the troops. For all intents and purposes the boys in blue were done with fighting.

Fortunately, Hooker realized the futility of deploying demoralized troops. Assuming command at the beginning of winter conveniently allowed him time to correct the problems and to prepare the army for the spring campaign.

His first move was to put a more liberal furlough plan into action. Two officers per regiment and two enlisted men per hundred would be granted ten days leave of absence until all had received a chance to go home. Soldierly skill and cleanliness were encouraged, as improvements in following the manual of arms and in personal hygiene also earned a man a chance to go on leave. Second, Hooker upgraded the rations from hardtack, salt pork, and coffee, to potatoes, onions, rice, and molasses. In the spring butter, eggs, and chickens already roasted were added to the fare. Ovens were built in every brigade, and quality soft bread replaced the all too familiar hard cracker. Hooker's actions gave back to the men their spirit and self respect and gave the Union back its army. By the time spring arrived, the troops were well fed, well clothed, and ready to fight.

Sallie's diet was never any better than that of her comrades. The health of the men had been threatened by prolonged poor diet, and Sallie likely had fared no better. Under such conditions she could easily have wandered to some nearby family and allowed herself to be treated to a better life for the sake of self-preservation. But loyal she was, and she stayed with her men for better or worse. Likewise, her boys obviously never considered for a moment giving her an "honorable discharge" for the purpose of having one less mouth to feed. A strong bond had developed between the 11th Pennsylvania and their dog.

As spring progressed, the Army of the Potomac prepared to move again. On April 8, 1863 the 11th marched from Fletcher's Chapel to Stafford Heights north of the Rappahannock and across from Fredericksburg. The men were ordered into parade formation and waited for a long time. Eventually the army marched in review. True to form, Sallie was in the lead of the regiment with her favorite colonel, Richard Coulter, who was now back in command. Sallie never failed to respond to the atmosphere and mood of the men. With head held high she reflected the renewed courage and pride of the soldiers. Nearing the review stand, the soldiers saw a tall man in a black frock coat standing before the officers–the president of the United States. President Lincoln occasionally saluted an officer whom he recognized and waved his hat to the enlisted men. When Sallie came into the president's view, he doffed his stovepipe hat in greeting to her. Sallie had given pleasure to a man who was heavily burdened with the decisions of war. Her importance to the morale of the regiment did not go unnoticed by the commander in chief.

Drills had been constant and any break in routine was welcomed. On Friday, April 13, 1863, a review of Brig. Gen. John C. Robinson's Division was scheduled, and the men were instructed to look their best. The 13th Massachusetts Regiment determined to comply. Their commander, Col. Leonard, was a stickler for detail and his men often appeared at battalion drill wearing paper collars and white gloves. Although these were correct items for dress uniform, most units dispensed with them. On this occasion the men of the 13th visited all the sutlers and bought up their complete stock of collars and gloves so that no outfit could outdo them in cleanliness and style. "The boys shined their buttons, brushed their coats, and blacked their boots."[6]

These preparations reached the ears of Col. Coulter, who was bound to have a little fun at the 13th's expense. On review day the

13th appeared in grand form, marching with shining rifles and the firm tread of those who feel superior. The 11th Pennsylvania appeared in the standard plain uniform–all except one of their members. With the reviewing officers and their staffs riding in front, Sallie followed, leading the whole division decked with a white paper collar around her neck labeled "13" and a white glove on every paw. It only took Sallie, one member of the 11th, to outshine the whole dog-gone 13th Massachusetts. Coulter's plan had been the best kept secret in camp. Roars of laughter went up and were heard long after the men broke ranks. Paper collars and white gloves were entirely dispensed with shortly afterward, although no official explanation was ever given.

After three months in camp the army was ready for action. The harsh March winds that had damaged huts and tents had also dried the roads. Robert E. Lee's army still held Fredericksburg and effectively guarded the route to Richmond. In late April Gen. Hooker left the First and Sixth Corps across from Fredericksburg to give the appearance of preparing to cross. He moved the rest of the army as rapidly as possible to the crossroads of Chancellorsville in an effort to outflank Lee. It almost succeeded, but Hooker hesitated and delayed at some crucial points while Lee effectively outmaneuvered him.

On May 2, the First Corps was ordered up from Fredericksburg and joined the Union right flank on May 3. The flag of the 11th Pennsylvania was carried by Corp. John H. M'Kalip. General Hooker held a well-fortified position south of the Rapidan and the Rappahannock Rivers but withdrew on May 4. The soldiers had fought well, but the general had lost the battle.

The 11th regiment formed the rear guard for the withdrawal and found itself again at the mercy of the soldier's old foe–the weather. Rain fell and the army trampled the ground into the consistency of freshly mixed mortar. For the rear guard it was another Mud March. Once more they bivouacked north of Falmouth, Virginia, where Sallie presented them with her third litter, seven pups. The event was entered in the Morning Report of May 20, 1863.

On June 11 came orders to prepare for swift march–all excess baggage to be sent to the rear. Sallie was not sent to the rear, however. Through all their battles her defiant barking had given her comrades encouragement. Sallie was not excess baggage to the men of the 11th.

On June 12 they marched toward Warrenton in sweltering heat. Now the tramping feet raised a cloud of dust that settled not only on every uniform and haversack, but in the hair and eyebrows of every man. They took on the appearance of an aged army. Chaplain William Locke said they looked like "a regiment of octogenarians instead of our stalwart Western boys."[7] Reaching Edward's Ferry on June 25, they crossed the Potomac River and stood again in Maryland. Locke observed that, "Not one single regret pained our hearts at parting with Virginia, and we shall be glad never again to set foot on her disloyal soil."[8] Their next line of march was toward Frederick, Maryland, and northward. Ahead lay Pennsylvania.

Captain John Overmeyer, a member of Company D, 11th Pennsylvania Volunteer Infantry. He was promoted to major on December 26, 1864.

CHAPTER SIX

"HOME SOIL"

As the 11th Pennsylvania crossed the line into their home state on June 30, 1863, they gave a rousing cheer. They camped for the night at the James Wolford farm on the Emmitsburg Road, where they were inspected and mustered for pay. Orders dated June 26 were read to the troops, announcing that Gen. George G. Meade, a Pennsylvanian, had replaced Hooker as commander of the Army of the Potomac. On hearing the news of Meade, the reaction of Clarence Bell of the 13th Massachusetts, as recorded in a letter to his sister on June 28, was prophetic: "The report tonight is that General Mead [sic] has got command of the Army of the Potomac..., SO LET JOHNNIE GRAYBACK BEWARE."[1] Rumors placed Lee's forces at Carlisle, York, and at Harrisburg. It was a perilous time to be under a new commander. William Locke wrote:

> There comes an hour in the experience of every soldier when he feels that victory depends not so much upon the commander as on himself–on his own fidelity to duty. Such an hour came for the Army of the Potomac, and every man was nerved for the work before him.[2]

On the evening of June 30 Gen. Reynolds of the First Corps ate his evening meal at Moritz Tavern, where he briefed Maj. Gen. Oliver O. Howard, the next in command. He spent the night at the tavern sleeping across four plank-bottom chairs.[3] Reynolds had given a pass to Jacob C. Shriver, a sixteen-year-old, requesting provisions for the general's breakfast and that of his staff. The lad's parents, Mr. and Mrs. Christian K. Shriver provided meat, potatoes, eggs, and bread the next morning at the Commons, one mile north of the tavern. Mrs. Alice Shriver helped to prepare the breakfast. The general, in appreciation, offered her five dollars. She declined, but he insisted, saying, "Take it, for I may not live to come back this way and reimburse you for your great kindness."[4]

On the morning of July 1 the 11th Pennsylvania, now part of the Second Brigade of Robinson's Division, marched at the rear of Reynolds' First Corps following the divisions of Wadsworth and Doubleday. The countryside was peaceful; to the men it seemed like

43

paradise compared to regions south of the Potomac where almost every acre had been destroyed by battle or used for the burial of the dead. The mountains and fruitful valleys of Pennsylvania were a welcome sight, but peaceful thoughts ended quickly when a burst of artillery sounded ahead. Leaving the Emmitsburg Road at the Codori farm, the division was ordered at double quick across the fields to Seminary Ridge. Brigadier Gen. Gabriel R. Paul's Brigade was erecting breastworks on the ridge as Coulter's 11th Pennsylvania arrived from the Emmitsburg Pike.

Confederate Gen. Robert Rodes' Division had come toward Gettysburg from the northwest on the Mummasburg Road. Seeing the vulnerability of the Union First Corps' right flank, Rodes placed artillery on Oak Hill and struck with an enfilading fire. In response Gen. Robinson ordered Gen. Henry Baxter of the Second Brigade to send two regiments forward to meet the challenge. The 11th Pennsylvania and the 97th New York Regiments were sent forth under Col. Coulter. Through deadly fire Coulter's men advanced in an effort to hold the extreme right of the First Corps and to close the gap between it and the left flank of Howard's Eleventh Corps, which was just arriving on the field. General Baxter, who had arrived with the remainder of his brigade, succeeded in holding against an attack by three Alabama regiments. In a hot clash with Gen. Alfred Iverson's North Carolinians the 11th Pennsylvania, the 97th New York, 83rd New York and 88th Pennsylvania regiments captured five hundred men–parts of three regiments of Gen. Iverson's Brigade. Despite this capture, the Confederate assault did not weaken. The battle raged as the line was held until mid-afternoon. As ammunition ran low, the wounded passed their cartridge boxes to the front and additional boxes were gathered from the dead.

In the charge against Iverson the flag bearer, Corp. John H. M'Kalip of Company C was severely wounded. The flag fell among some bushes, where it was finally discovered by Pvt. Michael Kepler of Company D, who carried it for the remainder of the battle.

Some time after three p.m. Col. Coulter's 11th Regiment, nearly out of ammunition, was ordered to withdraw to the support of Lieutenant James Stewart's 4th U. S. Battery B near the railroad cut. With Early's Division attacking from the northeast, Rodes' Division from the north, and A. P. Hill's forces massed on Herr's Ridge, the Union line was outnumbered and outflanked. The Union First Corps, which had been fighting since morning in the brutal July heat fell back toward Seminary Ridge. About 4 p.m. Gen. Abner Doubleday ordered the First Corps to fall back through town. All except Robinson's Division were ordered to retreat. Baxter's Brigade and Stewart's Battery were the last to leave the line, finally receiving orders to withdraw at about 5 p.m. The 11th was the last to leave their position. While other Federal units fled through town in confusion, Coulter's men retired in good order, firing as they went.

Earlier in the day the Lutheran Church on Chambersburg Street had been designated a hospital for Robinson's Division. Chaplain Locke observed:

> Basement and auditory, chancel and choir, the yard in front, and the yard in rear, were soon crowded with the brave men of the Second Division wounded and dying.... That retreat was not all confusion. The same noble corps that had so successfully maintained its ground...when resistance was no longer possible fell back in solid phalanx.... Shoulder to shoulder they marched rank after rank halting to fire upon the advancing foe, and then closing up again with daring coolness.[5]

The regiment had 212 men and officers when it entered the battle on Oak Ridge; when it reached Cemetery Hill it numbered 79.[6] Sallie was among the missing. Colonel Coulter was given command of the First Brigade in place of Gen. Gabriel Paul, who had been badly wounded. Coulter did not wish to be separated from the 11th and received permission to take them with him from the 2nd Brigade to the 1st Brigade.

Late in the afternoon of July 1 the brigade was moved to the left of the line, parallel to the Emmitsburg Road. They built breastworks and remained on the battle line overnight and throughout most of July 2. At seven p.m. they were moved farther to the left in support of Third Corps and were subjected to artillery fire, suffering heavy losses. At ten p.m. the brigade was again ordered into position on the Emmitsburg Road and was not relieved until daylight of July 3. When the Confederate artillery unleashed a heavy bombardment on the Federal line, the unit was moved to the support of Rickett's Battery in front of Cemetery Hill, taking artillery fire from two directions and infantry fire from the front.

One member of the 16th Maine witnessed an incident between Col. Coulter and his flagbearer:

> Tearing up and down the line to work off his impatience, Coulter suddenly drew rein and shouted, "Where in Hell is my flag? Where do you suppose that cowardly son of a bitch has skedaddled to? Adjutant, you hunt him up and bring him up to the front!"
>
> Away I went hunting for the missing flag and man and finding him nowhere, returned in time to see the Colonel snake the offender out from behind a stone wall, where he had lain down with the flag folded up to avoid attracting attention. Colonel Coulter shook out the folds, put the staff in the hands

of the trembling man, and double quicked him to the front. A shell exploded close by, killing a horse and sending a blinding shower of gravel and dirt. The Colonel, snatching up the flag again, planted the end of the staff where the shell had burst and shouted, "There, Orderly; hold it! If I can't get you killed in ten minutes, by God, I'll post you right among the batteries."

Turning to ride away, he grinned broadly and yelled to me, "The poor devil couldn't be safer; two shells don't often hit the same place. If he obeys he'll be all right and I'll know where my headquarters are."[7]

A few minutes later, Col. Coulter was badly wounded in the arm but did not leave the field and soon resumed command. At about 3 p.m. on July 3 the Confederate forces massed for a desperate attack, and the brigade moved under severe fire to the support of Gen. Winfield S. Hancock's 2nd Corps, meeting the force of Pickett's Charge. They remained on the line throughout the night and prepared for another attack which did not come. The sun rose on July 4 to reveal a field as bloody and as devastated as the fields of Virginia. The home soil they had just admired three days ago had become a vista of obliterated crops, wrecked equipment, bloody bodies and rotting horse flesh. The crackling of skirmish fire still broke the silence, but Lee's army was in retreat.

Sallie had kept up during the rapid march to Gettysburg and onto the field of battle. She barked her defiance as each side advanced and was driven back. As at Fredericksburg, Sallie became separated from her unit during the intensity of the first day's battle. She did not know where the men had gone, but she did know where they had been. She returned to the familiar ground of Oak Ridge. There she found her fallen comrades, licked their wounds and stood silent vigil over the dead. Captain Benjamin Cook of the 12th Massachusetts

Captain Benjamin F. Cook, Company K, 12th Massachusetts Volunteer Infantry. He found Sallie on July 6 on Oak Ridge.
(Civil War Library & Museum, MOLLUS, Phila., PA.)

was on provost duty searching for stragglers and prisoners when he found her on July 6. The dog was weak and lean after five days without food, but she would not desert her chosen post. Only after the wounded had been removed from the field did she permit herself to be taken to brigade headquarters and from there to her own regiment. All who knew the fury of the battle were amazed that she could have survived. Her habit of keeping her distance from the gray uniforms no doubt kept her inconspicuous. How she had endured the lack of water in the 87 degree heat, no one knows. Certainly her canine wisdom, bull terrier tenacity, and her devotion to duty were shown once again at Gettysburg.

On July 6 the 11th Pennsylvania marched southward and again camped for the night on the Wolford farm where the water of Middle Creek awaited the weary men. The next line of march was toward Middleburg, Virginia, and across Goose Creek, where a substantial stone bridge had once stood. "But our friends from Richmond, after they themselves had made a safe passage, turned round and destroyed it," wrote Chaplain William Locke.

> Nothing was left but for us to ford Goose Creek. With the water three and a half feet deep, the crossing was not made without the occurrence of many ludicrous scenes. Some of the men were content to remove only shoes and stockings; others doffed coat and breeches. Many more, discarding every particle of Uncle Sam's uniform, excepting the cap, undertook the transit in the uniform provided by nature. One missed his footing and became an involuntary immersionist. Another let fall the bundle of clothes he seemed most anxious to keep dry; or stepping into a hole, for a moment both man and bundle disappeared. Escaping all the perils by water, the first step up the slippery bank was often a false step, letting down the too confident soldier into a bed of soft mud, or sliding him back into the stream.[8]

The camp that night was in sight of the town of Middleburg, which seemed unusually quiet. It was discovered that between one and two hundred Confederate wounded from the Gettysburg battle were quartered there. With them were liberal supplies gathered in Pennsylvania and Maryland. General John Newton, who had commanded the First Corps after the first day at Gettysburg, ordered these supplies to be considerably lessened. Locke observed:

> It may be gratifying to some Pennsylvania farmer to know that a part of his smoked hams...is now filling the haversacks of Pennsylvania soldiers.[9]

The Union army saw duty north of the Rapidan River during September and October as the opposing forces maneuvered for key positions. Robinson's Division retraced many steps of the past two years at Warrenton, Bull Run, Thoroughfare Gap, Bristow Station, and Culpeper.

Camp life became a dull routine of drill, and evenings held little except cards, dice, or story telling. One popular tale about Sallie was written by Richard Coulter in an 1867 pamphlet:

> In pitching camp at the end of a day's march, the rabbits were frequently started up from their hiding places, and then a scene took place at once exciting and highly amusing. The poor rabbit, bewildered by the shouts of the men, would dash headlong, heedless of its course, Sallie close behind him at the top of her speed, the men increasing in numbers as the chase progressed, over stacks of muskets and piles of knapsacks and baggage, with shouts and cheers and laughter, through shelter tents, stopping for nothing; the rabbit eluding many a vain grasp to seize him and many a blow aimed at him with pick, shovel, musket, or club, through the regiment or brigade, twisting, turning and doubling until at length gaining the open field, he and Sallie would have a neck and neck race, out of which she always became the victor and the unlucky rabbit furnished a grateful meal for the fleetest soldier who was in "first at the death."[10]

Such light moments in camp helped to allay the anxiety of more battles to come. The Confederate Army and the elusive capture of Richmond still loomed. In late November Gen. Meade encountered the Army of Northern Virginia posted along Mine Run, south of the Rapidan River, and ordered his army to cross the river. Colonel Coulter commanded the division reserves–the 90th Pennsylvania, the 16th Maine, and the 12th Massachusetts. Major John Keenan was in command of the 11th Pennsylvania. The flag was still in the hands of Pvt. Kepler.

The weather was extremely cold. This was hard on all the troops, but was especially hard for those on picket duty where no campfire was permitted. Three pickets of the 11th froze to death at their posts. To make matters worse, the supply wagons were still on the other side of the river and the men were out of rations. A general withdrawal was ordered, and as the men marched back toward the river, the hungriest called out some offers for a piece of hardtack. Twenty-five cents was the first offer, then fifty cents. Finally one dollar was the offer, but even that high price brought none. Many a soldier remembered Fort Wayne and the bountiful baskets of the West Chester visitors–the cakes, pies, pickles, pickled eggs, apple fritters, boiled turkey, and apple wine. In those days they had so disdained hardtack that they had strung some pieces on a rope and hung the garland around the neck of the horse belonging to the regimental commissary. This was the ration that had just become so valuable a commodity. A ration of beef came on the second day, and the smell of beef and coffee in camp that night delighted every nose and palate.

General Meade could see no strategic advantage along the Rapidan and began to withdraw his forces to winter quarters. On December 4 the army forded the Rappahannock River, wading water three feet deep. The temper of the men was as hot as the water was cold. The names they devised for those in command of the army were vivid and decidedly unpleasant, although somewhat milder than they might have been had the men still been marching on empty stomachs.

Along the line of march they approached Cedar Mountain, where Sallie had first participated in battle. On this return visit Sallie gave birth to two pups. The morning report shows: "Sunday, December 13, 1863–Camp on Southbank Kelly's Ford, Virginia. Sallie–to camp, two pups which according to regulations have been named 'Rappahannock' and 'Rapidan.'"

The brigade was ordered to guard the heights of the mountain as the army proceeded. The weather remained as much an enemy as the Confederate Army. John Vautier of the 88th Pennsylvania regiment recorded in his diary:

> Saturday 2nd [January]–Very cold. Still on picket. The Brigade changed camp to the top of Cedar Mountain. Marching up the mountain we got orders to halt and rest and so cold was it that a man in the 11th Penna. was frozen to death in the few moments we halted."[11]

They finally encamped near Culpeper, and the men began to build substantial log cabins with fireplaces and chimneys. By good fortune Sallie and the pups, a short-haired breed, had outlasted the cold and the rigors of the march until the regiment was settled into camp. From the sweltering fields of Gettysburg to the freezing fields of Virginia she had been equal to a soldier's task and had endeared herself all the more to the men. The winter continued to be a bitter one, and this encampment ended all major operations in the East until Lt. Gen. Ulysses S. Grant arrived and launched the Wilderness Campaign in May 1864.

CHAPTER SEVEN

"WHIRLPOOL OF DEATH"

On January 5, 1864, the three year enlistment of the men in the 11th Pennsylvania expired. The war had outlasted their term of service, and the Union still needed them. After all they had suffered and endured, two hundred and four men still reenlisted–over three-fourths of the regiment. Because so large a portion remained in service, the proud regiment continued to exist. Their fighting spirit had kept the unit together; never was it dissolved or absorbed into another unit. They had started strong and would continue strong.

The reenlisted men were rewarded with a thirty-five day furlough. On February 5 they were sent to Alexandria, where they received pay and new clothing, then went on to Harrisburg. There they disbanded for their separate destinations: to the homes that would provide some well-deserved rest and the enjoyment of family and home cooking. Sallie made her second visit to Greensburg for another well-earned furlough.

During this period recruiting stations were opened at Pittsburgh, Greensburg, Lock Haven, Jersey Shore, Carlisle, and Mauch Chunk. When the regiment reassembled at Camp Curtin near Harrisburg on March 20, 1864, over three hundred recruits were present, bringing regimental strength to five hundred and ninety. By April 3 they were in camp at Culpeper reorganizing and drilling, as part of the Fifth Corps, Robinson's Division, and Gen. Baxter's Brigade with Gen. Gouveneur K. Warren commanding the corps. At this time Pvt. Kepler became ill, and the flag was delivered to Corp. J. J. Lehman, of Company D who carried it through the Battle of the Wilderness.

The First Corps's Second Division, of which the 11th was a part, once was recognized by an adversary. Dr. Hayes of the 88th Pennsylvania, taken prisoner on July 3, 1863, was met on the Gettysburg battlefield by General Richard Ewell and questioned as to what division he was attached. Hayes replied that it was the Second Division of the First Corps, whereupon Ewell "allowed that it was the best fighting division of the Army of the Potomac."[1]

Grant's strategy was to drive aggressively for Richmond. In early May that drive began. The Army of the Potomac again crossed the Rapidan and advanced toward the Wilderness in an effort to turn Lee's flank. William Locke described the Wilderness: "Never was a dreary and desolate belt of country more properly named. It is a region of dense woods, not of large trees, but of gnarled and ill-shapen oak so thickly studding the ground, which in many places is broken and marshy, that a man could hardly march through it without trailing his musket."[2] The Fifth Corps spent the night at the crossroads near the Wilderness Tavern, where a quiet dread, a solemn sadness, settled over the camp. In the stillness the men could hear a distant rumbling that told them that the Army of Northern Virginia was moving to meet them.

The Federal forces opposed Ewell's Corps on the morning of May 5. In the midst of furious fighting both sides became entangled in the Wilderness. Colonel Coulter's horse was shot. Men could not see their own units and could not maneuver together. Regiments, brigades, and even divisions were mixed. The dry underbrush caught fire and many wounded burned to death. Only night brought a halt to the horror, and stretcher bearers worked throughout the night to carry out the wounded.

On the following morning all forces of both armies were committed to action and the battle raged all day. General Baxter was wounded and carried from the field, leaving the command of the brigade to Col. Coulter. Major Keenan was in command of the Eleventh. In the afternoon Gen. Longstreet moved his Confederates against Hancock's Second Corps in the most fearful attack of the day and one which threatened the Union left. Coulter was ordered to move his brigade to the aid of Gen. John Gibbon's Division along the Brock Road. Colonel Coulter had yet another horse wounded, and Maj. Keenan's horse was killed. By night both sides were firmly entrenched with neither holding an advantage. Scattered along the way from Brock Road to Wilderness Tavern lay one hundred fifty-seven dead and wounded of the 11th Pennsylvania.

Corporal Philip K. Faulk wrote a detailed description of the Battle of the Wilderness:

> During the latter part of April, 1864, the Eleventh Pennsylvania Regiment was in camp near Culpeper, Va. About that time a number of regiments were detailed in a body to throw up entrenchments. While engaged in this work it was generally surmised that it was done as a feint to deceive the enemy, whose camps were in full view of the ridge that was being fortified.... In the event of an assault [it] would have proved a most formidable means of defense.

Late in the afternoon of the 3d of May, 1864, while many regiments were engaged in brigade drill upon the open fields, aides galloped from headquarters to the commanders of brigades and divisions. Orders were communicated to colonels of regiments and then transmitted to captains of companies. Immediately the long bristling blue lines filed briskly toward their camps. Meade's stirring address had been issued. It was the bugle note of an advance once more upon the vigilant and active foe. Immediately upon our return to our quarters six days rations were issued, with orders to march precisely at midnight. Quietly the rations were distributed without unusual commotion, for peremptory orders had been given to preserve the greatest quiet and secrecy and that no other than the usual camp fires be kindled.

Long before the hour of twelve had arrived all was in readiness–every knapsack was packed and every musket stacked in its appropriate place. Many of the men were asleep. Others stood or sat around the smoldering embers that yet glared brightly when fanned by the chill night wind. As the hour of twelve approached the hum of voices increased, knapsacks were slung and all the accouterments of the soldier hurriedly gathered up. The murmur of many voices, momentarily increasing in volume, was borne to the ear from near and far. Like the "resurrection of dried bones" prostrate forms suddenly became again inspired with life and rose up to take their places in the line. Impatience was visible in the features and manifest in the conduct of all.

"Twelve o'clock! Fall in, Fall in" rang firmly from line to line and was obeyed with an alacrity produced by unbounded zeal and confidence in our new leader General Grant. A hasty farewell glimpse of our deserted camps, and the long, dark columns toiled rapidly onward through the darkness toward the Rapidan. For more than three hours the incessant tread of thousands of feet pressed the moist soil until the cool breezes of approaching dawn found us far to the left of Pony Mountain. As the light of day grew brighter, the movements of our little army were apparent to all. For miles away to the left the long lines of the Second Corps were pressing forward, while the beams of the rising sun, scintillating upon their polished steel, added to the splendor and magnificence of the scene. Looking toward the front, our own Corps filled the roads and fields for miles, and in the rear and on our right Sedgewick's [sic] veterans came surging on in dark blue masses like the rapid gathering of clouds before the hurricane.

At 10 o'clock on the morning of the 4th Germania Ford on the Rapidan was reached. The river was here spanned by pontoons, over which a continuous stream of infantry, cavalry and artillery was passing. The yellow-colored earthworks on the south bank lay grim and silent; not an enemy was in view and not a shot was fired or any attempt made to dispute our passage. Upon gaining the south bank the troops bivouacked in line and thus waited several hours until our entire army, with the exception of Burnside's corps, had crossed the river. The scene here presented was one most imposing and magnificent. A large open space stretching far off to the left was covered with lines of blue bristling into thousands of flashing bayonets. From the distant woodland in the east, skirting the view, gleams of light, glinting the polished steel, told of the armed hosts that were there wheeling into line.

Our army was now in the vicinity of the famous Wilderness, a large tract of land embracing an area of many thousand acres, covered with a dense forest and penetrated by two main roads—the Orange Turnpike and the Orange and Fredericksburg plank road. In many places the tangled underbrush was absolutely impassable, and in two others the low swamps and pools of stagnant water were concealed by tall, dead weeds. Lee's advance was moving rapidly up on the two roads with intention of confronting us amid the labyrinthine mazes of the dark and tangled Wilderness. The enemy, no doubt, expected to repeat here the story of Chancellorsville and send our pierced and broken lines back in rout and defeat.

At 5 o'clock on the morning of the 5th our lines were again in motion. In our front rumbling sounds were continually heard, announcing the near approach of an eager and expectant foe.... In the afternoon our advance reached the vicinity of the Wilderness Tavern. Ewell's Corps had reached Parker's Store and its advance division were already in line of battle, when the Sixth Corps hurried to its place on the right and Hancock's Second Corps threw out its veteran lines on the left. These movements, quickly made but without confusion, alone indicated that "the battle was on." Our artillery unlimbered and wheeled into position and other grim preparations were made all along the line.

The noonday sun poured down from a cloudless sky. Scarcely a breath of air stirred the opening forest leaves and the birds had ceased their twittering in field and glen. Nature seemed awed into silence by the ominous gathering of battle clouds. Only the fresh green blades of grass and the first flowers of spring seemed unchanged amid the intense excitement of the scene, and though trod to the earth, buried and broken, they yet perfumed the air with fragrant odors.

Suddenly the boom of artillery opened on our left, quickly succeeded by the rattle of musketry. A scene of wild excitement was visible away down the long line that reached far back into the hidden depths of the Wilderness. Brigades and divisions instantly swung into line of battle and advanced, or formed in column by division en masse and waited in reserve. Wadsworth's and Griffin's divisions of the 5th Corps moved forward to the attack gallantly and steadily, driving the enemy's advance back on the reserve. While thus in flush of triumph heavy Confederate reinforcements arrived, and our lines were in turn compelled to give way before a fierce and overwhelming charge. Our brigade (Baxter's) at once moved in quick time to the extreme right to support the wavering lines of the two divisions and to resist the further advance of the exultant foe, who, with their battle yell ringing out wildly above the hideous roar, were pressing forward with desperate bravery.

While advancing we caught a partial view of the struggle in which Wadsworth and Griffin were engaged. Clouds of cannon smoke slowly lifted from the trembling earth in front, while numerous wounded were streaming back to the rear. Among the first who emerged from the front was a stalwart lieutenant, who moved silently but bravely towards the rear with a ghastly bullet hole through his face just below the eyes from which a crimson stream had issued, leaving its gory traces upon his fine but dusty uniform.

Almost immediately after gaining the position aimed at the Confederate advance was checked, all was again silent, save the thunder of the enemy's batteries planted in the rear of their strong infantry columns. Suddenly the storm of battle broke out afresh in the Wilderness on our left, its thunders reverberating for miles along the expectant lines. It was evident that Lee was trying to turn Warren's left flank before Hancock with his right wing could effect a junction. Hill's Corps was making a violent effort to force Hancock's lines back to the river. Amid the smoke and dust that half concealed the stirring drama thus opened, the sun was sinking low in the west. The chill dews of night were already falling when Baxter's Brigade and Griffin's Division were ordered to the left to the support of Hancock. These orders were at once obeyed, and while the incessant and appalling roar of musketry on our extreme left increased every moment, our columns, moving by the right flank, pressed forward rapidly toward the scene of battle. While crossing the open field intervening between Warren's left and Hancock's right, the scene was grandly impressive. The pale green verdure carpeting the fields contrasted beautifully with the long blue columns winding along like huge serpents ready to strike quick and deadly blows. No stirring strains of martial music rang out in the calm evening air. The tattered bullet-torn colors of each regiment alone fluttered gracefully above the serried lines as if no scenes of carnage had ever stained their crimson stripes or blotted their silver stars.

As our lines at length entered the edge of the forest the most deafening cheers resounded far through the depths of the woodland. The enemy had buried themselves daringly against Hancock's right wing and were struggling fiercely and desperately to force their strong masses into the gap between Hancock and Warren. "Forward! Double quick!" fell from the lips of determined leaders. Our lines rushed forward still farther into the deep forest, growing darker into the falling shadows of night. On pressed our brigade, on through the stifling Wilderness with irresistible impetuosity and desperate courage. The Confederates at length retired from our front, falling for support upon a stringer line entrenched behind formidable breastworks constructed of logs, from which they poured upon our advancing lines a most galling and destructive fire. Darkness increasing, the musketry fire at length ceased, save the occasional reports, shrill and clear, of the picket's rifle.

Our brigade had lost heavily in killed and wounded. Night, with its kindly curtain, terminated the carnage and veiled in silence and darkness the living and the dead. Both armies rested upon the field. Our lines now extended along the Germania Ford and Chancellorsville Road, with the right resting near the Brock Road leading to Spotsylvania. During the night it was decided to make a simultaneous attack on the enemy's left by Sedgwick and on the right by Hancock. These dispositions made, the earliest dawn of day was appointed as the proper time to make the assault. In the dim gray of morn the lines were almost noiselessly formed; not a sound was heard save the rattle of plated accouterments and the ring of steel. Everything in nature surrounding us was dark, solemn and awe-inspiring. An almost noiseless advance began. At first slowly, but gradually quickening, our long line at length burst upon the enemy. So sudden had been our onset that even the vigilant enemy were taken by surprise. They had scarcely time to fire a single volley [before] our lines had captured their first line of breastworks.

Though the victory here was complete, there was no halting. Our excited lines continued to press forward into impetuous bravery. The dust and smoke of battle half blinded us and effectively concealed from view the Confederate's second line of entrenchments. Hurtling bullets alone served to remind us of the deadly proximity to a desperate foe. After advancing half a mile beyond the captured breastworks our lines were halted and the men ordered to lie down to avoid as much as possible a murderous fire of musketry poured in at short range from rifle pits and breastworks. While thus situated the Confederates suddenly poured upon our recumbent files a fearfully murderous volley. The effect was electrical; our entire line, with the exception of the killed and wounded, rising at once to repel the attack. It was a moment of deadly peril and wild excitement. The air was hot with hissing bullets.

An involuntary glance along the line revealed the most fearful carnage I had ever beheld. Amid the fire flashes and smoke of thousands of rifles, it seemed as if more than one-half our line had gone down like stubble before the tongue of fire. A solid sheet of death, red hot as a flame from hell, darted upon our ranks that shook in the fearful agony like a forest in the grasp of the tornado. The roar of battle swelled in volume, while mingling with the loud thunder was heard the wild battle screams of the enemy and the deeper cheers of the Federals. A noisome stench of powder smoke rendered the air hot and heavy. The groans of the wounded and dying were smothered by the thunders of battle and the fierce cries of the living that rolled along six miles of battle lines.

Murky clouds of dust and smoke rose up through the light spring foliage of the forest, shrouding in deeper gloom the awful scene. No martial music rang out to inspire with ardor and enthusiasm the two hundred thousand men who faced death for hours beneath the deep shadows of those dark woods. Like two opposing waves the hostile lines surged forward until mingles into one, then rolled back only to gain force to dash again into the whirlpool of death.

Early in the day Hancock's Corps drove back the enemy's lines like scattered chaff. In Warren's front the contest was stubborn and terrible, no decided advantage being gained by either side. The Sixth Corps sustained its position by the most obstinate courage. Hancock's lines, having exhausted their ammunition, fell back to the position occupied in the morning.

The Confederate forces, largely reinforced, had closed en masse and hurled their veteran columns upon Hancock's advance with resistless impetuosity. Thus the battle continued, neither army being able to flank or pierce the unconquerable lines of the other.

Our regiment, the Eleventh Pennsylvania, had already lost more than three hundred men, many of them new recruits. Generals Wadsworth and Rice had fallen and General Alexander Hays, former Colonel of the Sixty-third Pennsylvania Volunteers had received a bullet through his brain. Thousands of the bravest in the ranks had died and were scattered over the field like withered autumn leaves in the track of the north wind. In the breastworks captured by our lines in the morning the dead of friend and foe were intermingled, as if they had fallen interlocked in deadly hand-to-hand encounter. Knapsacks, blankets, cartridge boxes and muskets were also scattered in all directions. The trampled underbrush and splintered trees gave evidence of the terrific storm of battle and blood that had so recently swept through.

In the field hospital of the First Division of the Second Corps more than two thousand lay wounded and dying. A continued stream of faint and bleeding humanity was pouring back from the reeking front. Amputating tables groaned with fainting sufferers and the surgeon's knife was plied unceasingly. The scene was sickening and terrible, even as much so as the awful carnage of battle which still raged on like a carnival of hell not two miles distant.[3]

This was Faulk's last battle. A rifle ball had shattered his elbow, necessitating the amputation of his arm.

Among the soldiers were many relatives–brothers, cousins and even fathers and sons. In Company B of the 11th were a father and son, John and Sam Edgar. According to family history Sam lied about his age to join the regiment on March 1, 1864. His father became concerned, joined on March 23, and followed him. He did not catch up to the regiment until April 10 at the encampment near Culpeper where he found Sam in good spirits. Sam's letter to his mother on April 12 stated, "Papa and I tented together. I think there will be a move made shortly, for the sutlers are all ordered to the rear and I think this will end the war and we will be home to take Christmas dinner." Sam prepared for the future when he wrote a letter to his mother on April 23, asking her to arrange the purchase of land for him for after the war.

John Edgar wrote frequently and told his wife on March 31: "Enclosed you will find a finger ring which I want you to wear for my sake as the words is on it, 'Forget me not.'" He wrote on April 23 that, "Samuel and me gets along first rate. He is as fat as a bear. He enjoys himself better than I do. I get downhearted sometimes for it is so very long between letters."

Both John and Sam were wounded during the Battle of the Wilderness. Neither came home for Christmas. Mrs. Edgar received a letter from 1st Sgt. H. Truesdell written on June 7, 1864: "Your husband, Edgar was wounded on the fifth of May in right leg a little below the knee. His wound was not considered dangerous. He was sent to Washington and I suppose is there now in hospital. Your son Sam was wounded at the same time through the left breast and died about three days after. He died on the way to Fredericksburg." According to the sergeant, Sam was buried by his own men somewhere between Chancellorsville and Fredericksburg. Another account of what happened comes from family oral history. They believe that John was captured, was in Libby prison and died the day of release, falling about a block away. Supposedly he was buried under a tree there. His leg injury had become infected and probably gangrenous.

On the evening of May 7 Gen. Warren was ordered to move on the Brock Road toward Spotsylvania Courthouse in an attempt to seize the high ground. The 11th was in the lead on the all night march where men stumbled along in the dark and some fell asleep while marching. The exhausted soldiers went directly into battle at daybreak with the Southern forces already in command of the best ground and Hood's veteran division in front of them. General Robinson was severely wounded and was carried from the field, leaving Col. Coulter in command of the division. Major Keenan, leading the 11th and cheering them on, was shot and killed. Sallie was hit in the neck by a minie ball. The wound was examined and bandaged by the field surgeon, who sent her with other wounded back to the hospital. There she was carefully reexamined by Dr. Chase, who pronounced that the wound was not dangerous but that the ball could not be removed. She remained at the hospital for a short time.

As the regiment continued in the struggle for Spotsylvania its ranks were terribly thinned. Lehman, still bearing the flag was killed. The flag was brought off the field by 2nd Lt. M'Cutchen of Company F. The next color bearer, unnamed, was badly wounded in the foot. Corporal William Mathews of Company C carried the flag for the remainder of the engagement. Robinson's Division had lost its commanding officer, all the brigade commanders, and two thousand officers and men. The division was temporarily broken up and reassigned, Coulter's Brigade moving to Crawford's Division. Advancing on Laurel Hill under heavy fire and holding the hill for five hours until being relieved, the brigade suffered 229 casualties out of its nine hundred men. In a later attempt to carry the higher ground, Col. Coulter was wounded in the chest and carried from the field. Sallie returned to the front still carrying her painful burden.

"I propose to fight it out on this line if it takes all summer," stated Gen. Grant. The bloodshed did indeed continue throughout the summer and into the following spring.

Chapter Eight

Taps

The North had been drafting men since the summer of 1863, just after the Battle of Gettysburg. While most were good soldiers, some reluctant conscripts gave the group the reputation of running from the face of the enemy. Back on the field after her hospital stay, Sallie had an encounter with one such reluctant conscript. Frightened by enemy fire, the man broke ranks and was in retreat. Sallie's comrade from the 12th Massachusetts described it: "She did much to check desertion. It is a well known fact that the first thing a great many conscripts did after joining the army was to run away. One tried this in the Eleventh. Sallie saw him when he started and interrupted his game by planting her teeth firmly in his flesh, thus reminding him of his duty to his country."[1]

For several months Sallie carried in the fleshy part of her neck the minie ball which had hit her at Spotsylvania. It became enclosed in a cyst and could be felt inside a lump the size of a hen's egg. Eventually this festered, and the minie ball dropped out, leaving behind a well defined scar. Through all this time she remained active and faithfully carried out her soldierly duties.

General Grant was determined to get around Lee's forces or to defeat Lee before he was forced into the formidable entrenchments around Richmond. Consequently, Grant continued to order movements to the left in an effort to reach the rail center of Petersburg, south of Richmond, and cut Lee's supply lines.

The 11th was glad enough to leave the dreary area of the Wilderness and Spotsylvania and felt temporarily refreshed by marching through beautiful Caroline County, which was untouched by the war's ravages. Their route led south to the North Anna River and Jericho Ford. The flag was now carried by Corp. William Matthews of Company C, who continued in that duty through December 1864. He was then relieved by Sgt. Albert Carter of Company A.

Chaplain Locke remembered that, "Time was when the first thing to be done after a halt was to make coffee.... Now the first thing the men do is to entrench."[2] At Jericho Ford they had just entrenched when a heavy assault was made on the center line. This was repulsed and one thousand prisoners taken in the action. Still, the Union was unable to take the Confederate position, and after two days of fighting they crossed the North Anna by night and proceeded to the Pamunkey River. There pontoon bridges were ready for their crossing, and the Army of the Potomac again stood on the York peninsula where it had been in 1862.

The Federal troops continued marching by night and fighting by day. The Confederates remained unconquerable. The men of both sides were unspeakably weary. Union soldiers wrote their names and regiments on paper and pinned or sewed them inside their jackets in hope of at least being identified when dead. In June Grant sent his army toward Cold Harbor, a crossroads eight miles from Richmond, in the midst of the creeks, gullies, and swamps between the Pamunkey and the Chickahominy Rivers. Lee's forces arrived there first and dug in. It became a battle of trenches and frontal assaults fought to a bloody stalemate. Both armies remained in the sweltering and stinking trenches for ten days, when Grant secretly moved his army out by night and sent it to cross the James River and to attack Petersburg. Siege warfare had begun.

The lines at Petersburg were about one hundred yards apart. Men and officers lived in "bomb-proof" quarters and moved through "covered ways." Sharpshooters picked off everyone who showed himself above the earthworks. In August the Fifth Corps was ordered three miles southward to seize the Weldon Railroad, a major supply line for Lee's forces. Warren's Fifth Corps succeeded in tearing up more than a mile of track before being engaged by A. P. Hill's Corps. Crawford's Division on the right was almost outflanked but rallied to the charge of Baxter's Brigade, and the Union line held.

From May through winter losses on the battlefields, skirmishes, on picket and in the trenches totaled one hundred thousand men. The organization of single regiments, indeed the entire army, was radically changed. Five hundred men had been lost to the 11th Pennsylvania during the campaign. New recruits coming rapidly to the front assured the 11th of maintaining at least two hundred members. With many new faces the "Old Eleventh" was hardly recognizable.

On December 7 an attempt to gain further control of the Weldon Railroad was undertaken, as the Confederates were shipping supplies on the southern section of track and from there to Petersburg by wagon. This attempt to destroy the railroad fell on Warren's Fifth Corps, the Third Division of the Second Corps, and Gregg's Cavalry. The 11th participated in the destruction of twenty miles of railroad. Ties were burned and heated rails were bent to resemble the badge of the Fifth Corps, the Maltese Cross. Rails on Southern lines were usually made of iron rather than steel and could vary in strength from 16 to 68 pounds per yard. A length of rail could be heated in the center and then bent around a telegraph pole to the desired shape.[3] Locke observed: "The burning ties, aided by the nearest fence rails, cast a lurid light on the midnight heavens, telling the Confederate Commander...by whom the ruin was wrought." The Hicksford Raid brought about the complete destruction of the Weldon Railroad. Barely escaping a planned ambush by Confederates, the Federals returned northward. They had marched one hundred miles in six days. Overnight the ground froze hard; the surrounding forests yielded logs for the construction of cabins for winter quarters.

Richard Coulter remembered: "During the operations on the Weldon Road, the Hickford raid, and siege of Petersburg Sallie traveled along, or stayed with the men in the trenches or in the forts, or on the picket line, always at her old place at the head of the column when it moved, announcing the departure by barking and jumping at the horse of the officer in command."

In early February came a warm breeze from the south and daily inspections–signs of an early campaign. A fierce bombardment of Confederate lines on the evening of February 4 preceded troop movements the following morning. The Fifth and Second Corps marched all day on the 5th and bivouacked at Dabney's Plantation.

On the night of February 5 Sallie chose to sleep in the tent of a sergeant and three men of Company D. Her behavior that night was not as usual. Throughout the night she wakened them with pitiful cries. They chased her away several times, but she persisted, returning with moans and howls. Always the one to give joy and comfort to the men, Sallie now seemed to need comfort or consolation. Her behavior proved to be prophetic.

The next day Sallie again led the men into battle, and fell victim to a Confederate bullet. She was found lying with the bodies of the sergeant and one man of Company D, with whom she had spent her last night. The two others who had shared the quarters were severely wounded. The official record stated: "'Sallie'" was killed when Regiment was making its first advance upon the enemy the 6th instant–she was in line with the file closers when shot. We buried her under the enemy's fire." One of the men in a letter dated "Camp near Hatcher's Run, Va., February 11, 1865," wrote: "Poor Sallie fell in the front lines in the fight at the Run–a bullet pierced her brain. She was buried where she fell by some of the boys, even whilst under a murderous fire."[4] Samuel Bates also spoke of "a faithful dog which had followed the Regiment through all its campaigns, always taking its place beneath the flag in battle."[5]

The regiment retreated to the breastworks that night. It was their first night without Sallie. Some men were only then learning of her death. Battle weary men lacked her comforting presence, her settling down in someone's tent, her licking of faces. Her life had been completely molded by army routine and events. Sallie had been with them through the worst and the best of times. Now they would finish the war without her.

By morning the Union continued its thrust westward until on February 10 Hatcher's Run was secured. The battle extended the Union line westward by two miles, giving the beleaguered forces of Robert E. Lee thirty-seven rather than thirty-five miles to defend. Grant's noose continued to tighten around Petersburg and Richmond.

For several days in mid-March the troops had been preparing for a review. President Lincoln and a party of ladies and gentlemen from Washington, guests of Gen. Grant, were to review the army before returning to the capital. General officers had sent to City Point for the dress coats and fancy horse trappings which, having no practical use in battle, had been left there earlier. The enlisted men wore whatever the quartermaster could supply. They shined their muskets and rubbed brass plating to a silvery brightness. Early on the morning of March 25 troops wakened to the sound of gunfire. Experienced ears knew that it was not a morning salute. Instead of the expected order to fall in for review, Gen. Crawford's headquarters received the order to fall in for battle. Soon the troops were moving quickly to the right. The Confederates had captured Fort Stedman to the east but their success was short-lived. All points of the Federal army rallied and pushed the victors back over the space which they just gained. Caught in the cross-fire of artillery to the right and left of Fort Stedman, the Confederates had no choice but to surrender. His only escape routes lay to the west and north. Crawford's Division marched back to its place on the Union left.

Another general move was soon underway. When the order came on March 29 there was nothing to indicate that this would be the army's last campaign. The men had long given up speculating on whether each campaign might be the last. Locke recorded, "Passing by the cooking apartment of regimental headquarters, a soldier struck his musket against the cracker box set up on a barrel to help the draught of the chimney. 'Don't knock dat chimbley down, please sah,' said the cook. 'We'll be back here agin in a week, and I'll want to use it.'" But he was a false prophet. This was the regiment's last move from the old camp near the Jerusalem Plank Road. At 3 a.m. the Fifth Corps was moving in the direction of Dinwiddie Court House. Grant's objective was to seize the Southside Railroad and the crossroads at Five Forks ten miles north of Dinwiddie Court House. This would block Lee's only chance of escape.

General Philip Sheridan's Cavalry, which had joined Grant's forces after the defeat of Early in the Shenandoah Valley, was ordered to attack the enemy's right. Crawford's Division was on the Halifax Road with Baxter's Brigade in the rear. At one time the 11th could have made a show of resistance equal to a brigade. Now neither volunteering nor drafting could fill the ranks to more than a fourth of their original strength.

By noon the troops had reached Quaker Road and crossed Gravelly Run, where Warren's Fifth Corps established a battle line approximately three miles, as the crow flies, from Five Forks. Griffin's Division was on the right, Ayers in the center, and Crawford on the left. By evening Coulter's Brigade had a strong line of entrenchments across the Boyden Plank Road. General Lee had issued orders that Five Forks must be held at all costs. With heavy reinforcements from Petersburg, Lee was personally directing operations against the Union front. The Confederates drove Ayers back in confusion. Crawford's lines also went down in the assault falling back upon Griffin's position. After four hours Warren's complete Fifth Corps reformed and advanced, driving the Confederates back and capturing almost the entire Fifty-Sixth Virginia Regiment with its complete stand of colors.

Meanwhile, on March 31, Sheridan's Cavalry, trying to hold Dinwiddie Court House found the enemy too strong and was driven back. The Fifth Corps, sent to reinforce Sheridan, was in battle position shortly after noon on April 1. Their advance had been slow over roads heavy with mud; the men had been worn down by four nights of marching and battle. Locke paid tribute to the men:

> But they were doing all that men depending on their own legs alone could do, and when they merged out into the open ground upon which they were to act, the compact lines of the old Fifth Corps told that the lessons learned in the van of many important army movements since the crossing of the Rapidan a year before were not quite forgotten.

Crawford's Division was on the right of the line. The difficult nature of the ground–bogs, tangled woods, and pine thickets–threw Crawford too far to the right, a lucky mistake. Griffin was able to fill the gap between Ayers' and Crawford's Divisions. Crawford's wheel to the left brought him up behind the enemy. Once through the thick woods and bushes, Ayers charged the enemy at close range and, joined by Griffin, both divisions swept down the Confederate line toward Five Forks.

In the final charge the 11th Regiment of Baxter's Second Brigade found themselves close to their old commander "Dick" Coulter leading the Third Brigade. As Coulter's men overran a Confederate battery of four guns, the 11th joined them in a rousing cheer. In his exuberance over victory, Sgt. H. A. Delavie of Company I snatched the flag of the 32nd Virginia Regiment from its retreating bearer and waved it triumphantly over the captured works. By seven o'clock p.m. on April 1, burning campfires were surrounded by groups of jubilant boys in blue.

Richmond was evacuated on April 2. Before dawn on April 3 Lee had withdrawn northward from Petersburg across the Appomattox River. On April 9, 1865, Robert E. Lee surrendered his army to Ulysses S. Grant, and on April 26 Gen. Johnson surrendered to Gen. Sherman. The war was over.

At Appomattox the Union Army, with the exception of the Fifth Corps, began to pull away. Chaplain Locke observed: "We confess to a feeling of loneliness, as with the disappearance of the last brigade over the hill that bounded our view, the notes of fife and drum, every moment growing fainter, were heard no more." In the following five weeks the terms of the surrender were carried out and the last Southern soldier paroled. Then the bugle sounded the order for the homeward march. As Harrisburg had been the gathering place for departing regiments, so it would now become the gathering place of those returning. The old 11th Pennsylvania would be scarcely recognizable as the regiment that left there in 1861. Of the three thousand men enrolled in its ranks during the war less than three hundred marched back to Camp Curtin. Only Gen. Coulter and one or two of the original staff officers remained to identify the regiment.

Following the suggestion of the Secretary of War, Edwin Stanton, Federal troops marched in review in Washington before being mustered out. On May 23 and 24, 150,000 officers and men passed in parade formation. The city was profusely decorated for the occasion, and vast crowds of people gathered to honor the veterans at this, the Grand Review. Triumphal arches were erected, and people along the street placed garlands of flowers upon the tattered uniforms of the men. Cheers and patriotic songs mingled with the loud tramp, tramp of the marching men. They marched, not with the weariness of the last four years, but with the step of victory.

Following the cavalry and the Ninth Corps came the Fifth Corps with Crawford's Third Division last in line. Its Third Brigade was led by Col. Richard Coulter, now Breveted Brigadier General Coulter. Sergeant Albert Carter of Company A carried the tattered remnant of the state flag as he had at Weldon Railroad, Hatcher's Run, Five Forks, and Appomattox. All flags were draped with black crepe on the flagstaff in mourning for President Lincoln. The flag of the 11th was different. They had outlined the center red stripe with strips of black crepe and edged the flag with black as well. This was their special tribute to Abraham Lincoln.

Upon the main reviewing platform stood Gen. Grant and President Andrew Johnson with other officials, but Lincoln's familiar face was not among them. The History of the Grand Army of the Republic stated:

...the marching soldiers missed above all others that rugged, homely face which would now have been lit with a halo of glory. The great patient heart that for four years had borne such a fearful strain, was now stilled. In all the land no one was nearer the soldier's heart than Abraham Lincoln.

But the thoughts of the soldiers were not then so much with the absent leaders as with the more familiar forms of comrades, dear to their hearts, but now numbered with the dead. Perchance they had been playmates in school-boy days and bosom friends in [their] maturer years. Together they had responded to the call of an imperiled country, together they had faced the dangers of the service. In camp and bivouac they had slept under the same blankets and shared the contents of their haversacks and canteens.... Never could they forget the sacred bond of comradeship welded in the fire of battle.[6]

To the men of the Eleventh Pennsylvania Volunteer Regiment the poignant memories included one special comrade. How Sallie would have loved this parade! That she was sorely missed is reflected in the poetry and articles written by comrades not only in the 11th, but also in other regiments. One comrade wrote:

There is nothing now to mark the spot where she fell, no stone or tablet to her memory, her grave is–

In the distant dell 'neath protecting trees,
Where the streamlet winds and the violet waves,
And the grasses sway to the sighing breeze.
But in the long after years when the gray-haired
Veteran of the war for the Union
Repeats the legend of his earlier days, he will tell
His listening grandchildren the story of Sallie.[7]

And the veterans did just that, for personal accounts of Sallie were shared with the younger generation by aging veterans who attended the fiftieth anniversary encampment at Gettysburg. In memory's eye they still held the stirring image of a colonel, a flag, and a dog.

CHAPTER NINE

BEYOND THE SMOKE OF BATTLE

Colonel Richard Coulter

At the conclusion of the war Col. Coulter returned to Greensburg and continued in his law practice. He married Emma Welty and they raised a family of two girls—Rebecca and Margaret—and four boys—Richard, Henry, Alexander, and William.

Coulter invested in and promoted the coal mining industry in Westmoreland County and served twenty-seven years as president of the First National Bank of Greensburg. He remained a prominent citizen until his death in 1908. Throughout his postwar years Coulter was instrumental in placement of veterans in soldiers' homes and in securing pensions for them. He always loved dogs, and he never forgot Sallie. The earliest publication about Sallie—the 1867 pamphlet—is attributed to him by a Westmoreland County historian. A similar article in an 1885 edition of *The Bivouac* states "written at the request of Richard Coulter."

Coulter was born in Greensburg on October 1, 1827. His father was a well-known businessman and his mother was the daughter of John Alexander of Carlisle, a colonel in the American Revolution. Richard studied at Jefferson College at Canonsburg, Pennsylvania, now Washington and Jefferson College, completing his work in 1845. He next entered the law office of his uncle, also named Richard Coulter, but left in December 1845 when he first heard the call to military duty. He enlisted in the Westmoreland Guards militia, which was considered to be an elite unit.

When the Mexican War began in 1846, the militia unit became Company E Second Regiment Pennsylvania Volunteers. Coulter was a nineteen-year-old private when his unit departed for active duty on December 30, 1846. The regiment was transported from Greensburg to Pittsburgh and then down the Ohio and Mississippi Rivers by steamboat. Coulter recorded in his daily journal his life as an enlisted man.[1] Of his first experience with hardtack, Coulter remarked, "Supped this evening on government regulations.... Sea biscuits are perfect jaw-breakers, especially after the soft raised bread of a Pittsburg hotel." After leaving New Orleans, he wrote that, "Our provisions have been very bad for some days back. Crackers perfectly green with mould, pork rancid and almost solid fat, occasionally a light streak of lean like a small cloud in a clear sky."

The company's first action in Mexico was at Vera Cruz, where a siege lasted until spring. Coulter's notes of March 31 read: "This afternoon overhauled my knapsack, washed all my clothes, and am now ready for the march inland. This I look upon as one of the ugliest jobs of the campaign, to bend over a half barrel wash tub in the hot sun and rub a lot of dirty shirts, socks, and red drawers until one's hands are completely cramped and wilted." On April 28 he wrote: "Mess cook today...rained heavy...had flour rations to bake and wet wood to bake them. Attempted to make pancakes...by the time I had a few baked my batter was reduced almost to the consistency of water by the rain." On the march toward Mexico City Coulter made this entry; "To the stream this morning before daylight for water, stepped too close, and went into some three feet of mud and water. Not having time to dry myself or wash the mud and gravel from my shoes, had quite a disagreeable march."

In September the army assaulted the castle at Chapultepec; Coulter, now a lieutenant, was in command of the company. First Sgt. Thomas Barclay, also of Greensburg, recorded in his journal that, "Coulter wheeled our company and we rushed directly up the hill which was very steep...By this means, Company E was first...in the castle."[2] By late May the armistice had been ratified by Mexico and troops moved out on June 1, 1847. Coulter and his associates reached Pittsburgh on July 11 and returned to a festive welcome in Greensburg. He had been engaged in all the principal battles fought by Gen. Scott's column. At the conclusion of that war he resumed the practice of law until duty again called him.

Richard Coulter's rise through the ranks molded not only his military prowess, but also his empathy for the common soldier, and prepared him for the gallantry he was destined to display in the American Civil War. When the 11th Pennsylvania was organized for three-month service, Coulter took his old company of the Mexican War into that regiment. He organized the 11th when it began the three-year enlistment and became its commander. He earned the nickname "Fighting Dick" and was twice honored by brevet: breveted brigadier general for gallantry at the Wilderness and Spotsylvania Courthouse in August 1864, and breveted major general for gallant conduct at Five Forks and in the assault on Ford Road in April 1865. He was wounded at Fredericksburg, Gettysburg, and Spotsylvania.

The tributes paid to Coulter by his comrades give a measure of the man. John Stulen on the 90th Pennsylvania Regiment, part of Baxter's

Brigade, said of him: "We boys of the 90th took quite a fancy to Colonel Coulter. I remember him as a soldier with a determined spirit. While a man of strong language, he was always ready for a fight, a brave officer without any frills." Stulen told how Coulter was wounded at Spotsylvania:

We, after a hot march, arrived in the afternoon and took our position in the line of battle. The losses had been heavy on both sides and...the dead still lay on the field where they fell, including many artillery horses, and the stench was horrible. The rebels were strongly entrenched in our front and the musketry and cannonading was very brisk. I noticed an officer coming toward us alone.... As he came near, say about 300 feet from our line of battle, I could hear him shout, "Give them ____ boys!" I looked back through the smoke and recognized General Coulter, who had come out alone to encourage us, at a great risk, as it afterward proved. A short time later, on looking back I saw him fall. I quickly laid my gun on the ground and ran toward him. He was lying on the ground severely wounded in a very exposed location. The rebel yell at that moment seemed to be getting closer. I partly carried, partly dragged him a short distance to a safer location. While trying to make him as comfortable as possible I stooped down and asked him if I could do anything more for him. He said, "No," and immediately added, "I have an aunt at home praying for me." It was only a short time after that when some staff officers came and had him carried off the field, and I returned to the position I had left.[3]

Major Joseph B. Rosengarten, writing in *General Reynold's Last Battle*, said, "Dick Coulter was never in battle without leaving his mark." Captain Henry B. Piper, in dedicating the regimental monument at Gettysburg said, "While the records of the Commonwealth endure, Pennsylvania will do well to honor the name of General Richard Coulter. Wounded again and again, with indomitable courage and endurance, he led the old Eleventh gallantly in all its fights. Cool, brave, even-nerved, well-balanced, self-poised, he possessed the highest instincts of a true soldier, united with the manliest attributes of a true man. Long may he live to meet and mingle with the survivors of that gallant band he so often led to victory and never deserted in defeat."

The body of Richard Coulter was laid to rest in the St. Clair Cemetery in Greensburg, Pennsylvania, on October 14, 1908, with survivors of the 11th Pennsylvania serving as pallbearers. An unnamed comrade who wrote to the editor of the *National Tribune* on the occasion of Coulter's death said, "With all his wealth [he] was a plain, modes, unobtrusive citizen, a friend as true as steel, and one of the fiercest enemies imaginable [on the field]. It is said of him that he never flinched from any public duty nor failed in a private obligation."

The Colors

John C. Scheurman of Company A was the last color-sergeant and carried the flag from May 28, 1865, until the regiment was mustered out. On July 4, 1866, he formally presented the colors to the governor of Pennsylvania upon the occasion of the return of all state flags. The regimental colors now repose in the care of the Pennsylvania Historical and Museum Commission and the Capitol Preservation Committee in Harrisburg, Pennsylvania, where all the regimental flags are being restored.

Repairs to the colors had begun long before the end of the war.

The battered remnant of the 11th state color vividly illustrated the pride which the rank and file attached to their flag. Rather than request a replacement flag from the state, the men resolved to keep their original, battle-worn banner. At least twice during the war, the regiment authorized emergency re-

The tatered remains of the 11th's battle flag. It has since been restored.

(Capital Preservation Committee)

pairs to the flag. The first evidence of this occurred on September 8, 1863, when the regimental council of administration authorized that a part of the tax assessed on the sutler be used to make repairs to the flag."[4]

A similar measure was adopted on April 29, 1864. The flag shows what these repairs entailed. Replacement silk was obtained and sewn directly to the remnants of the original stripes. The added silk supporting the shredded original stripes is thought to be of a different composition as evidenced by the differential aging and fading of the two materials.[5]

The national flag that was captured by the 17th Virginia at Second Manassas was retaken at the end of the war. It was finally returned to Pennsylvania in 1905.

During the existence of the regiment there were twenty-one flag bearers, one whose name is not known. Two of the twenty-one carried the flag off the field after the bearer fell. Only three were killed while carrying the flag. Corporal William Mathews carried the colors unscathed for seven months and six engagements: Spotsylvania, North Anna, Cold Harbor, Bethesda Church, Petersburg, and Weldon Railroad. Mathews was mortally wounded at Hatcher's Run and died a month later.

The Liberty Tree

In Annapolis, Maryland, the tree where Sallie had her first pups still stands on the campus of St. John's College. Now believed to be approximately four hundred years old, the towering tulip poplar is the second oldest tree in Maryland. Its name, Liberty Tree, is derived from its use as a rallying place for the Sons of Liberty who, like their Boston counterparts, staged a tea party and burned the British ship the *Peggy Stewart*. Under its branches strolled George Washington, Lafayette, and Francis Scott Key. Many 4th of July picnics were held there during the nineteenth century. Since 1929 it has been silent witness to the commencement exercises of the college.

During its long life the tree has survived many hazards. In 1840 some school boys exploded two pounds of powder in its cavity, inadvertently benefitting the tree because an infestation of worms was destroyed. In 1848, it was accidentally set on fire but was saved by the efforts of many townspeople. By 1887 the trunk had become a mere shell. In 1907 the cavity was expertly filled, a task requiring fifty-five tons of concrete reinforced by iron and steel. In 1975, a wind storm opened a six-foot-long crack in the ninety-six-foot tall tree. Some limbs were trimmed and repairs were made. Careful maintenance has continued to keep the Liberty Tree growing and healthy.

St. John's College

St. John's College, chartered in 1784, is a direct descendant of King William's School, which was founded in 1696. Its first building, presently known as McDowell Hall, is the one in which the 11th Pennsylvania was quartered during the Civil War. The college did not operate during the war years, and in addition to quartering Union regiments it housed Union men recently exchanged for Confederate prisoners, and served as a hospital. The buildings of the college suffered extreme damage during this time. The government paid $4,666.00 in damages, but the board had to borrow $11,500.00 to complete the repairs.

McDowell Hall on St. John's campus which housed the 11th PA.
(Photo by Shirley Cubbison)

Gettysburg Campsites

The Wolford and Shriver farms where the 11th Pennsylvania camped before and after the Battle of Gettysburg are located in what is still a rural area, through which Middle Creek and Marsh Creek flow peacefully. Traces of an eighteenth century mill can still be discerned in the Middle Creek stream bed. A dilapidated smokehouse is the only farm building remaining. The Moritz Tavern is still in use as a private home.

William H. Locke

After serving as chaplain of the 11th Pennsylvania for three years (1862-1864), William Locke returned to his civilian ministry and served with distinction until his retirement in 1904. Counting both civilian and military time, he served for 52 years as a pastor.

Born in Baltimore, Maryland on March 28, 1826, William was six years old when his family moved to Pittsburgh, Pennsylvania, traveling over the mountains in a wagon. As a young man, he learned the printing trade but soon felt called to the ministry. He was admitted to the Pittsburgh Conference of the Methodist Episcopal Church, now United Methodist, in 1852 and served in Butler, Wilkinsburg, Birmingham, and South Pittsburgh, Greensburg, Lawrenceburg, and Braddock. In Greensburg, he met and married Margaret Loor. They were the parents of six children, three boys and three girls. Two of his sons entered the ministry.

After his Civil War service Locke returned to the Pittsburgh area and for a time taught English literature at Beaver College. He continued to be interested in higher education and served on the Board of Control of Mt. Union and Beaver Colleges. Returning to the ministry, he was assigned to Sewickley, Pittsburgh, and Beaver. When the Pittsburgh Conference was divided, he moved to the newly-created Ohio Conference and served at Alliance, Canton, Youngstown, Cambridge, New Philadelphia, East Liverpool, Barnesville, and Cadiz. He was presiding elder (district superintendent) of the Akron District for four years, was conference secretary, and in 1884 was a delegate to the General (National) Conference. While at Cadiz he was appointed chaplain of the State Reformatory at Mansfield, a position which he held for eight years. At Canton he received the honorary degree of Doctor of Divinity. Canton was the home church of President William McKinley with whom Dr. Locke developed a friendship that lasted until the death of McKinley.

William Locke died on June 15, 1905, and was buried at Sewickley, Pennsylvania. The *Western Christian Advocate* of June 21, 1905, reported: "Dr. Locke was one of the most scholarly and accomplished members of the Conference to which he belonged. The literary style and finish of his sermons was exceptional, and his voice rang true to all the great moral doctrines of the Church, to whose service he gave his long life." His daughter, Miss M. Katherine Locke, writing in a history of the East Liverpool church, said:

> In East Liverpool, as in all others of our homes, my father's pulpit was his throne. He so combined in his sermons his ripe culture, his deep spiritual nature, his keen study of the trend of the events of the day, that he interested young and old in the different walks of life. Father knew men and he loved men. He

knew how to approach men, to mingle with them, and to attract them to his church. He identified himself with all social and civic interests of East Liverpool. He was an ardent patriot, and was a conspicuous figure in all national celebrations. Having been a chaplain through the Civil War, father was a personal friend of the old soldiers.

The words of Locke quoted frequently in this volume bear out the qualities cited by his daughter. His deep feeling for the common soldier made him a great humanitarian. His expression of their feelings and grasp of each situation would be lost without quoting him. He presents the comic, the tragic, and the dedicated service of the men. *The Story of the Regiment* is both a tribute to the men and a literary legacy.

Colonel Phaon Jarrett

Respect for Col. Phaon Jarrett was not limited to the 11th Pennsylvania Volunteers. His contributions as a mathematician and civil engineer won recognition from all his associates. His selfless nature was consistent throughout his life.

Phaon Jarrett was born on February 9, 1809, in Allentown, Pennsylvania. He was educated at a Moravian school in Bethlehem, Pennsylvania. In 1828 he received an appointment to the U. S. Military Academy at West Point, where he had high scholastic achievement. After three years he had to return home to manage his father's estate. He read law with a notable attorney and was admitted to the bar of Lehigh County. His skill as a director of public works was widely known, as was his work on many railroads in Pennsylvania, New York, and New England. He was especially noted for his contribution in the construction of the Philadelphia and Erie Railroad.

As an "earnest and sincere Democrat"[6] he had little sympathy for either side in the "political phase which induced the War Between the States."[7] However, when the integrity of the North was threatened, he organized a company and marched his men to Harrisburg. Besides instructing in the camp at West Chester he also taught military tactics at Harrisburg and Pittsburgh.

Jarrett's military skills soon came to the attention of Gen. Patterson, and the 11th became one of the units first ordered to the field when combat was expected. This was the case at Falling Waters, where the 11th was in the advance. At the end of the three-month enlistment term, with "an immediate attack still threatening, Col. Jarrett induced his force to remain in the field until all apprehension had subsided."[8]

Due to his rigid political connections no future military appointment was offered him. Jarrett died at Lock Haven on September 16, 1876, and was buried at Allentown. He was praised as a public-spirited citizen, a lover of his country and of justice, unselfish, and a true friend.

General Robert Patterson

After leaving military service, Gen. Patterson always felt that his reputation was marred by the accusation that, by retiring before Winchester, he had failed to hold Gen. Joseph E. Johnston in the Shenandoah Valley and to prevent Johnston from going to the aid of Beauregard at Bull Run. Because of this alleged failure, Patterson was relieved of his command of the Army of Pennsylvania on July 25, 1861, and was given an honorable discharge on July 27, 1861. He did, however, receive the support of his fellow officers, who praised him as a skilled military leader and a noble soldier.

Patterson felt the need to vindicate himself and sent a request to the secretary of war on November 1, 1861, citing the contradictory communiques he had received from Gen. Scott. Patterson's nine-point explanation was:

1. All his regular troops had been recalled to Washington, leaving him with no artillery and a single company of inexperienced cavalry.

2. Scott had ordered him back to Maryland after some of his troops had crossed the Potomac.

3. Patterson was ordered to advance while his command was in a crippled condition and was reinforced only after an advance would have been effective.

4. The General in Chief had never ordered him to do more than threaten the enemy at Winchester.

5. Had he been expected to follow Johnston closely toward Manassas he could not have done so, since the Confederates were moving largely by rail and Patterson's army by foot.

6. The General-in-Chief forbade pursuit of the enemy, in the event that he should retire towards Manassas, fearing to press him on Washington.[9]

7. Scott indicated that McDowell would move on Manassas on July 16 at which time Patterson was to advance upon Winchester. Patterson followed this order, but McDowell's movement on Manassas was not until July 21.

8. If his army had attacked Winchester on July 16, Patterson's defeat as well as McDowell's would have placed the Confederates at the front door of Washington.

9. General Scott had indicated that the enemy at Winchester was inferior, yet he knew two days after the battle of Bull Run that siege artillery three times heavier than Patterson's had been left by the Confederates at Winchester and a greater number of guns had been carried away.

After his request to the War Department was denied he appealed to the president. Having heard all the facts, President Lincoln said, "General Patterson, I have never found fault with you or censured you; I have never been able to see that you could have done anything else than you did do. Your hands were tied; you obeyed orders, and did your duty, and I am satisfied with your conduct."[10] While Patterson appreciated Lincoln's words, he still felt that a court of inquiry was needed to "stop the abuse daily lavished" upon him. He next appealed to Congress, but was told that because he had already been discharged there would be no court of inquiry. Lastly, he took his case to the public in *A Narrative of the Campaign in the Valley of the Shenandoah in 1861.*

Robert Patterson was born in Ireland on January 12, 1792. When he was a small boy his family came to America and settled on a farm near Philadelphia. As a young man he served in the War of 1812, rising to the rank of colonel of Pennsylvania militia and serving as a captain in the regular army. He was mustered out in June 1815 and returned to Philadelphia where he established himself as a grocer. In 1835 he traveled in the upper Mississippi and Iowa and later published his observations. He sat in the state convention of the Democratic-Republican party that nominated Andrew Jackson for president.

Serving in the Mexican War, he became major-general of volunteers and commanded a division at Cerro Gordo. He led the cavalry and advance brigades that took Jalapa and was honorable mentioned by General Scott. After discharge in 1848 he returned to business, becoming prominent in the development of the sugar industry in Louisiana. He also acquired interests in sugar and cotton plantations and eventually owned thirty cotton mills in Pennsylvania. He was a promoter of the Pennsylvania Railroad and of steamship transportation between Philadelphia and other ports. From 1833 until the beginning of the Civil War he commanded a division of Pennsylvania militia.

At the beginning of the Civil War he was mustered into Federal service as a major-general of volunteers and assigned to command the Military Department of Pennsylvania, Delaware and the District of Columbia, later called the Army of Pennsylvania. He returned to civilian life after the three months' service. Robert Patterson died in Philadelphia on August 7, 1881.

Despite all his efforts to maintain his credibility as a commanding general, history still records Patterson as being "duped" by Johnston. General Patterson's reasons for desiring vindication were not merely for himself but for the honor of his state, for those who served with him, and for his children and grandchildren.

Dr. James Anawalt

Doctor Anawalt was assistant surgeon with the 11th Pennsylvania from October 19, 1861 to October 26, 1862. After nine months with the 132nd Pennsylvania, he returned to the 11th as chief surgeon on May 27, 1863, and served with them until the regiment was mustered out on July 1, 1865.

Doctor Anawalt was a resident of Greensburg, Pennsylvania, and a graduate of Jefferson Medical College of Philadelphia. He practiced medicine for a total of thirty-nine years including his military service. The Westmoreland *Democrat* of September 2, 1896 stated that he "ranked high as a physician."

In 1886 Dr. Anawalt was paralyzed by a stroke and was in declining health for the next ten years. He resided with a brother in Scottdale, Pennsylvania for some time and then entered the National Military Home in Dayton, Ohio. Richard Coulter, in statements relative to Doctor Anawalt's admission to the soldiers' home, reviewed illnesses that Anawalt had suffered during the war. At Annapolis he was ill for three days in January, 1862. He was also ill for the month of April, 1864, at Culpeper, Virginia. When he died in Dayton in late August 1896 at the age of 68, Richard Coulter paid for the transportation of his body back to Scottdale for burial at Mt. Pleasant.

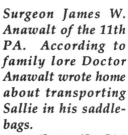

Surgeon James W. Anawalt of the 11th PA. According to family lore Doctor Anawalt wrote home about transporting Sallie in his saddlebags.

(Courtesy of Ronn Palm)

The Regimental Monument

A monument dedicated to the "heroic dead" of the 11th Pennsylvania stands on Oak Ridge in the Gettysburg National Military Park. Atop it is the bronze figure of a skirmisher preparing to fire. At the base of the monument lies the figure of Sallie. Both face westward across the grassy field toward Chambersburg. Because Doubleday Avenue runs behind the monument, a tourist can pass without noticing Sallie; but a patch of bare earth just to the front of the monument provides evidence that Sallie has not gone unnoticed. Guides are sure to point her out, and countless people have posed there for photographs, intrigued by the thought of a loyal dog so honored by her comrades. The sheen of the bronze on the head and back of the figure suggests that many a small hand has "petted" the dog.

This monument was dedicated on September 3, 1890. Captain Henry B. Piper gave the address. He stated in conclusion:

> But I cannot...forget the uncrowned and unsung hero of the knapsack and musket. History furnishes no parallel to the gallantry of our citizen soldiery, the courage and grit of the American volunteer. The perils and hardships of war were his. His were the lonely vigils of the picket beat, and the dangers by flood and field. Upon his brave heart and conscience lay the political destiny of this great republic. The nation placed her life in his hands. And on a hundred bloody battlefields he proved himself sublimely worthy of the trust. Among this unselfish host of brave, true men, none were more brave and true than the soldiers of the Old Eleventh. Their bones lie on every great battlefield of the east, and the records of southern prisons show the names of some of our gallant boys.... To him, the common soldier, to our dead comrades...we turn in grateful, tearful remembrance. We rear these monuments to their honor and in their memory. But in the unborn ages yet to come, long after we too shall have passed away, a saved and grateful republic will rear in history an everlasting memorial to their devotion and their valor, more changeless than brass and more enduring than marble. That shall exist as long as these voiceless hills bear testimony to Gettysburg's fateful day; and among the immortal names preserved as those the nation delights to honor in all the future, a high and honored place shall be forever held by the old "Eleventh Pennsylvania Volunteers."

ENDNOTES

Forward
1. Fort Sumter – 1861, 43. This shot is sometimes attributed to Edmund Ruffin, a sixty-seven year old secessionist who did fire a shot from another location, Cummings Point.
2. William E. Barringer and Earl Schenck, ed. *Lincoln Day by Day*, 59.
3. Frank Taylor, *Philadelphia in the Civil War–1861-1865*, 33.
4. *Ibid.*, 31.
5. *History of Lycoming County*, 433.

Chapter 1
1. Clinton *Democrat*, Sept. 21, 1876.
2. John Lippy, *Sallie the War Dog*, 18.
3. David Swisher, personal interview.
4. Samuel Bates, *History of Pennsylvania Volunteers, 1861-1865*, Vol. I., 43. A member of the 26th PA regiment was killed in Baltimore during the mob action of April 19, 1861, but not in battle.
5. Sauers, *Advance the Colors*, 63.
6. *OR*, Series I. Vol. 2, 168.
7. *Ibid.*
8. *Ibid.*, 169.
9. Bates, 106.

Chapter 2
1. Pension records, NARA, File #388.063.
2. Richard Coulter, "Sallie," 3.
3. "Soldiers' Faithful Dog, Sally," Gettysburg *Compiler*.
4. *Ibid.*
5. From the speech of Governor Andrew Curtin of Pennsylvania upon the presentation of all regimental colors.

6. "Soldiers' Faithful Dog, Sally," *Compiler*, Oct. 10, 1910.
7. Richard Coulter, "Sallie"
8. Bierer Papers, Pennsylvania Archives.
9. *Ibid.*
10. William Locke, *Story of the Regiment*. 56, 57.

Chapter 3
1. Phil R. Faulk, *The Battle of Cedar Mountain*.
2. John J. Hennessy, *Return to Bull Run*, 55.
3. Fletcher Webster letters, 12th Massachusetts files, USAMHI, Carlisle, PA.
4. Fletcher Webster letter, Sword.
5. Charles E. Davis, Jr., *Three Years in the Army: The Story of the Thirteenth Massachusetts Volunteers*, 63.

Chapter 4
1. Stephen Sears, *Landscape Turned Red*, 189.
2. John Brenahan, "Battle of Antietam," *National Tribune*.
3. Sears, 190.
4. *Ibid.*, 190.
5. *Battlefields of the Civil War*, 176.
6. John Lippy, *Sallie the War Dog*, 36.
7. William Locke, *Story of the Regiment*, 147.

Chapter 5
1. Locke, *Story of the Regiment*, 164, 165.
2. Coulter, "Sallie," 4.
3. Bruce Catton, *The Civil War*, 118, 119.
4. *Battlefields of the Civil War*, 197.
5. Dunkelman and Winey, *The Hardtack Regiment*, 44.

6. Davis, 199.
7. Locke, *Story of the Regiment*, 213.
8. *Ibid.*

Chapter 6

1. USAMHI, Carlisle Manuscript Archives, Carlisle, Pa.
2. Locke, *Story of the Regiment*, 225.
3. E. R. Shriver, family oral history.
4. *Ibid.*
5. Locke, *Story of the Regiment*, 231, 232.
6. *Ibid.*, 243.
7. Abner Small, *Voices of the Civil War*.
8. Locke, *Story of the Regiment*, 260, 261.
9. *Ibid.*, 261.
10. Coulter, "Sallie," 7.
11. John Vautier.

Chapter 7

1. Alfred Sellers, letter of July 9, 1863.
2. Locke, *Story of the Regiment*, 197.
3. Faulk, *Annals of the War*.
4. Edgar letters.

Chapter 8

1. "Soldiers' Faithful Dog, Sally," *Compiler*.

2. Locke, *Story of the Regiment*, 342, 343.
3. Douglas R. Cubbison, "Destruction of Transportation and Communications Infrastructure," 1.
4. Coulter, "Sallie," 6.
5. Bates, 265.
6. Robert Beath, *History of the Grand Army of the Republic*, 9.
7. Coulter, "Sallie," 8.

Chapter 9

1. Volunteers: The Mexican War Journals..., quoted by Robert B. Van Atta in "Greensburgers Chronicle Mexican War Duties," Greensburg *Tribune-Review*.
2. *Ibid.*
3. John Stulen, "Letter to the Editor," *The National Tribune*.
4. Sauers, *Advance the Colors*, 63.
5. *Ibid.*
6. "Death of Col. Jarrett," *Clinton Democrat*.
7. *Ibid.*
8. *Ibid.*
9. Robert Patterson, *A Narrative of the Campaign in the Valley of the Shenandoah in 1861*, 14.
10. *Ibid.*, 18.

BIBLIOGRAPHY

Baringer, William E. and Earl S. Miers., ed. *Lincoln Day by Day, A Chronology, 1809-1865.* Dayton, OH: Morningside, 1991.

Bates, Samuel F. *History of the Pennsylvania Volunteers, Vol. 1, 1861-1865.* Harrisburg, PA: B. Singerly, 1869.

Battlefields of the Civil War. New York: Arno Press, 1979. (Reprint of 1961 NPS Historical Handbook Series).

Beath, Robert B. *History of the Grand Army of the Republic.* New York: Bryan, Taylor and co., 1889.

Bierer Papers. Pennsylvania State Archives, Pennsylvania Historic and Museum Commission, Harrisburg, PA.

Brenahan, John. "The Battle of Antietam." *National Tribune.* Washington, D.C. Feb. 21, 1889.

Catton, Bruce. *The Civil War.* New York: The Fairfield Press, 1971.

Coulter, Richard. "Sallie." *Republican and Democrat.* Greensburg, PA, 1867.

Cubbison, Douglas R. "Destruction of Transportation and Communications Infrastructure." Madison, AL: White Star Consulting, 1996.

"Danville," Montour County Historical Society. H. B. Brower, ed. Harrisburg, PA: Lane S. Hart

Davis, Charles E., Jr. *Thirteenth Massachusetts Volunteers.* Boston: Estes and Lauriat, 1894.

"Death of Col. Jarrett." Clinton *Democrat.* Lock Haven, PA: Sept. 21, 1876.

"Death of Benjamin F. Cook." Gloucester *Daily Times.* Glouchester, MA: Sept. 3, 1915.

"Death of Doctor Anawalt." Westmoreland *Democrat.* Greensburg, PA: Sept. 2, 1896.

"Death of Gen. Coulter." *National Tribune.* Washington, D.C.: Oct. 29, 1908.

"Death of Rev. Dr. William H. Locke." *Western Christian Advocate.* June 21, 1905.

Dictionary of American Biography. Vol. XIII. Dumas Malone, ed. New York: Charles Scribner's Sons, 1946.

"Dr. Anawalt Dies." Greensburg *Tribune Herald.* Greensburg, PA. Aug. 29, 1896.

"Dr. Locke Dies in New York." The Pittsburg *Press*. Pittsburgh, PA. June 17, 1905.

Dyer, Frederick H. *A Compendium of the War of the Rebellion*. Vol. III., New York: Thomas Yoseloff, 1959.

Edgar Letters. Private collection of Norman Donovan.

Faulk, Phil R. "Battle of Cedar Mountain: What a Pennsylvania Soldier Saw and Heard on the 9th of August, 1862." Philadelphia *Weekly Times*. Vol. VIII. No. 6, Mar. 31, 1883.

Faulk, Phil K. "Annals of the War; Battle of the Wilderness." Philadelphia *Weekly Times*, Vol. VIII. No. 36. Oct. 25, 1884.

Fort Sumter - 1861. *Civil War Times Illustrated*. Special Issue XV. No. 6. Gettysburg, PA: Historical Times. Oct. 6, 1976.

Hawthorne, Frederick W. "Eleventh Pennsylvania Infantry." *Men and Monuments as Told by Battlefield Guides*. Gettysburg, PA: Licensed Battlefield Guides, 1988.

Hennessy, John J. *Return to Bull Run*. New York: Simon and Schuster, 1993.

Hunt, Roger D. and Jack R. Brown. *Brevet Brigadier Generals in Blue*. Gaithersburg, MD: Olde Soldier Books, Inc., 1990.

Kollar, Robert R., "On Their Own Ground: The 11th Pennsylvania Regiment at Gettysburg." *Westmoreland History, Civil War issue*. Greensburg, PA; Westmoreland County Historical Society, 1995.

Kretschman, E. A. *Letter to Col. J. P. Nicholson*. Philadelphia, PA: Sept. 8, 1890.

"The Liberty Tree." pamphlet by St. John's College, Annapolis, MD.

Lippy, John D. Jr. *Sallie the War Dog*. Harrisburg, PA: Telegraph Press, 1962.

Locke, M. Katherine. "Pastorate of William Henry Locke, D. D." *Memories*. Metsch and Boyce, eds. East Liverpool, OH.

Locke, William Henry. *Story of the Regiment*. New York: James Miller, 1872.

Lycoming County, History of. John Meginness, ed. Chicago: Brown, Runk, and Co., 1892.

Methodism in Western Pennsylvania. Wallace Guy Smeltzer, D. D., ed. Little Valley, NY: The Straight Publishing Co., Inc., 1969.

Morning Reports, Eleventh Pennsylvania Volunteers. Greensburg, PA: Westmoreland County Historical Society.

Nicholson, John P., ed. *Pennsylvania at Gettysburg*. Vol. II. Harrisburg, Pa: William S. Ray, 1904.

Official Records. Series I. Vol. 2.

Partridge, Eric. *Dictionary of Slang and Unconventional English*. 7th ed. New York: McMillan, 1976.

Patterson, Robert. *A Narrative of the Campaigns in the Valley of the Shenandoah in 1861*. Philadelphia: John Campbell, 1865.

Pension Records, National Archives, Washington, D. C., File # 388.063.

"Reverend Dr. William Henry Locke." Obituary. The Pittsburgh *Bulletin*. June 17, 1905.

Rosengarten, Joseph B., "General Reynolds' Last Battle." *Annals of the War*. Dayton, OH: Morningside, 1988.

Sauers, Richard A. *Advance the Colors! Pennsylvania Civil War Battle Flags*. Harrisburg, PA: The Capitol Preservation Committee, 1987.

Sears, Stephen W. *The Landscape Turned Red*. New York: Ticknor & Fields, 1983.

Seller, Major Alfred. July 9, 1893: Gettysburg National Military Park, Vertical File: "90th PA."

Shriver, E. R. *History of the Shriver Family*. privately printed.

Small, Abner. *Voices of the Civil War*. Alexandria, VA: Time-Life Books.

"Soldiers' Faithful Dog, Sallie." The Gettysburg *Compiler*. Oct. 19, 1910.

Stulen, John. "Letter to Editor." *National Tribune*. Dec. 17, 1908.

Swisher, David. 11th Pennsylvania Reenactment group. Personal Interview. 1995.

Sword, Wiley. *Letter by Fletcher Webster*. Private collection.

Taylor, Frank H. *Philadelphia in the Civil War–1861-1865*. Philadelphia, 1913.

Vautier, John. Papers of The 88th Pennsylvania. U. S. Army Military Institute, Carlisle, PA.

"A War Dog." *The Bivouac. Independent military monthly*. Vol. III. Boston: Jan. 1885.

Volunteers: The Mexican War Journals of Private Richard Coulter and Sergeant Thomas Barclay, Co. E, Second Pennsylvania Infantry. As quoted by Robert B. Van Atta in "Greensburgers Chronicle Mexican War Duties." *Tribune-Review*. Greensburg, PA: Nov. 10, 1991.

Webster, Fletcher. Letter in 12th Massachusetts file, U. S. Army Military Institute, Carlisle, PA.

ABOUT THE AUTHORS

Shirley Evans Cubbison is a retired teacher, having taught language arts, American history, journalism, and creative writing. She has co-authored *Working Water*, a history of grist mills in western Pennsylvania, and is the author of *Andy Over the Schoolhouse*, a study of 43 one-room schools in Butler County, Pennsylvania. Since she belongs to a family of "Civil War buffs," entering this area of writing seemed a natural move.

Cindy A. Stouffer took an interest in the Civil War about ten years ago. Soon after moving to Gettysburg she initiated and chaired the committee for the erection of a monument in honor of Gettysburg's unknown soldier. She co-authored *One Soldier's Legacy*, the story of how interest in a soldier's identity led to a home for war orphans, the National Homestead at Gettysburg. During a tour of the Gettysburg Battlefield looking for human interest stories, Cindy learned of the popularity of the story of "Sallie." While working as a research assistant at the Cyclorama Library of the Gettysburg National Military Park she began her research of the regiment and its mascot determining to give it a wider audience.